SOUND
WAVES

SOUND
WAVES

By David Colley

St. Martin's Press
New York

Design by Doris Borowsky

Library of Congress Cataloging in Publication Data

Colley, David.
Sound waves.

1. Huber, Mary Ellen.   2. Children, Deaf—
United States—Biography.   3. Deaf—Means of
communication—Case studies.   I. Title.
HV2534.H8C65   1985   371.91′2   85-11769
ISBN 0-312-74607-5

First Edition

10 9 8 7 6 5 4 3 2 1

To Mary Liz

whose love and support
made it possible

Acknowledgments

I wish to express my grateful appreciation to Joan and Dick Huber and Claire and Jim Davis for the many hours they devoted to this book. Special thanks must be given to Mary Ellen Huber and David Davis for their efforts in helping me understand the nature of deafness. Thanks also to Helen Beebe and the staff of the Beebe center as well as to Donald W. Shive, president of the center's board of directors, his wife, Louise, and Thille and Geoffrey Newton.

—David Colley

Introduction

IMAGINE FOR A MOMENT that you are the parent of a profoundly deaf child and you learn of a pioneering teaching method that could enable your child to grow up a "hearing," "speaking," and socially adjusted adult. Would you choose this approach for your child?

Each year thousands of parents, some by choice, most because they are uninformed, reject such an opportunity. Instead, they enroll their children in programs that emphasize sign language, finger spelling, and lipreading as methods of communication. These children are destined to hear only partially, if at all, and to speak and be understood with difficulty. Many can communicate only with their deaf peers and are comfortable only within their own ranks.

Parents who are told their children are deaf experience an overwhelming sense of despair. Where can they turn for help? How can they tap the potential that lies locked within their children's brains? Instinctively they recognize that deafness strikes at the roots of intellectual development.

The manual methods of communicating are gaining wide

acceptance and popularity in the United States today. The ubiquitous deaf interpreter on television is but one example. The availability of books on the art of signing is another. The manual methods are taught from the assumption that profoundly and severely deaf children cannot learn to hear and speak. In fact, most education programs for the deaf de-emphasize or ignore the development of hearing and speech, in large part because the teachers do not believe that stone-deaf children can be taught both. In consequence, the bulk of graduates from the nation's schools for the deaf hear poorly, if at all, and speak with little melody and fluency.

In the last forty years, however, pioneers in the field of deaf education have demonstrated that deaf children can acquire normal speech and language by focusing solely on the development of hearing. At an early age these children are equipped with powerful hearing aids and "taught" to hear over a period of years. The results are so revolutionary that many teachers of the deaf, accustomed to using other methods, refuse to believe that these "auditory" children trained to hear are, in fact, profoundly or severely deaf.

The thrust of this unique method is the development of that small remnant of residual hearing found in all but a few deaf children. Use of visual or tactile modes of communication—lipreading and sign language—is discouraged. Years of training in listening skills enable the deaf child to develop speaking skills, clumsy at first, but near normal later on. Generally children so trained are easily "mainstreamed," and able to attend regular schools beginning at the nursery level. They are assimilated into society easily and unobtrusively. They are unaccustomed to being a part of the handicapped world.

Sound Waves is the story of a mother's struggle to bring

her daughter into the world of the hearing against the advice of all but one woman, Helen Hulick Beebe, a speech and hearing specialist in Easton, Pennsylvania. Beebe assured Joan Huber, a young mother from Allentown, that her profoundly deaf daughter, Mary Ellen, would grow up in the hearing world, learn to speak and develop just like any normal child. There was no magic or quackery in Beebe's belief. She had practiced it on a few children in the previous twenty years, learning the method in New York from a Viennese-born physician. The essential ingredient of the unisensory method employed by Beebe, so named because it concentrates on the hearing sense alone, is work and discipline for both parent and child. Joan Huber never ceased in her efforts to teach Mary Ellen to hear and to speak. Doctors and educators scoffed. Others warned of dire emotional consequences. Joan Huber persisted. This is her story.

1

A SMILE BROKE ACROSS the doctor's face as he examined Joan Huber's arm. He had seen classic examples of German measles before, but most had involved children.

"You're a little old for this, don't you think?"

Dr. Robert Rank was a pleasant-looking man, a general practitioner in his early thirties, who had interned in Allentown and decided to settle there. Like many medical residents who stayed on, Dr. Rank thought Allentown was an ideal spot to raise a family. It was clean, solid, and of manageable size, an All-American city, its residents liked to boast. Within a few miles of the downtown was the lush, green, and rolling Pennsylvania Dutch countryside, dotted by stone barns with hex signs to ward off evil. The Pocono Mountains were within an hour's drive, and New York and Philadelphia were within easy commuting distance.

Dr. Rank had known Joan for several years. His office was downtown, several miles from the Hubers' brick house on Troxell Street and, with two small children, they were frequent patients. Kathy was just two months old, Michael, two years, and they wore Joan to a frazzle.

Joan had been terribly tired the last few days, but didn't think much of it. She kept moving, assuming it was tension and exhaustion. How could anyone feel up that week? The entire Huber clan—Joan, her husband Dick, Mike and Kathy, and Joan's parents—had planned a trip to New York the weekend before to visit Aunt Helen. Joan and her mother were doing some last-minute shopping that Friday afternoon when the news came through that President Kennedy had been assassinated.

"Oh my God!" Joan exclaimed, almost in tears. It was a cold, gray November day, and suddenly everything seemed dead. The traffic moved more slowly as they drove home. The grass was brown; the leafless trees stood out against the somber sky. Joan had a particular affinity to the slain president. Her maiden name was Kennedy and she was a strong Irish Catholic.

The trip was postponed, and several days later Joan noticed a rash, pink at first, then turning bright red. Soon it covered her body, but she dismissed it as a nervous reaction to that long weekend. The television blared from dawn till past midnight, a constant barrage of voices, muffled drums, horses' hooves on macadam, volleys of rifle shots, and the nasal, slow drawl of the new president.

Joan listened between housecleaning, cooking, and diapering. Kathy cried constantly and Michael never stopped running, here, there, into this and that. Joan watched the news reports as she prepared for the usual family Thanksgiving feast.

"What a terrible week!" Joan thought. She was exhausted but managed a smile. No doctor had confirmed it but she knew she was pregnant. This was number three coming up. She wanted four.

The rash affected Joan's vanity more than her stamina, and she would have ignored it all and gone to New York with the family had her mother not insisted, "I won't go to New York with you unless you see a doctor." They had just finished their morning cup of coffee. Grandmother Kennedy lived two blocks away and dropped by almost daily to chat with Joan in the kitchen alcove or help with housework.

"Mom, that means an extra trip before the weekend. I'll go when I get back."

"I'm not going until you have seen the doctor," her mother persisted.

"It's only a rash. It's not going to kill me."

"Joanie, you don't know what it is and I want you to find out."

"You should talk," Joan replied as she rose to rinse the dishes. "You wouldn't see a doctor if you had to."

"Don't you worry about me," Grandmother Kennedy said. "You just see a doctor."

There was a warning in her mother's voice that prompted Joan to call for an appointment with Dr. Rank. As she dialed she looked out the window into their post-World War II neighborhood of small single-family houses and wide streets lined by poplar trees. A few blocks to the east, Allentown merged with the city of Bethlehem, known for its sprawling steel works. A mile or so to the north was Route 22, a four-lane expressway that cut in and out of the Pennsylvania and New Jersey hills on its way to New York. Joan drove in the crisp, early December air to Dr. Rank's office. The closer she got, the more she worried.

"So what is it today, Joan?" Dr. Rank asked after his nurse

had shown her into his office. "You didn't bring your rascals so you must be the one feeling under the weather."

He rose and motioned Joan toward the examining table.

"Come on and sit up here," he said. "How's Dick? I haven't seen him in a while."

"He's fine," Joan replied as she sat down.

"Now, what's the problem?"

"Some kind of nervous rash," Joan said feeling sheepish. It seemed insignificant.

"Well, let's have a look," he said.

""How old are you now, Joan?" Dr. Rank asked as he examined her arm.

"Twenty-seven."

He studied the gaunt, tired face and looked into the eyes that seemed deeper that day. She was classic Irish—angular features, sharp nose, jet black hair cut short and pixielike, and deep blue eyes. Fatigue dampened the luster of her eyes a bit. It was not a serious illness, and he smiled.

"I wish I had a picture of you for a book." He took Joan's arm and studied it again. "I hope you're not pregnant."

His words momentarily stunned Joan. For an instant she tried to comprehend the significance of his statement. It was his tone that concerned her. She knew little about medicine. As a girl her contemporaries played nurse and dreamed of becoming Florence Nightingales. Joan was not interested. Other mothers might have been alert to the symptoms of various illnesses, but Joan wasn't.

"Why?" Joan asked, her voice quiet.

"You have rubella."

She wasn't sure what that meant. She'd heard of German measles. That was something you were supposed to get as a child and if you came down with it as an adult everyone laughed just as Dr. Rank had done. But she didn't under-

4

stand why it was important not to be pregnant. She looked at Dr. Rank for reassurance.

"I think I *am* pregnant." She paused, waiting for his response. "What will it do?"

Dr. Rank frowned.

"How sure are you?"

"Pretty sure."

"That's not good."

"Why not?"

"It's just not good." He turned and walked back behind his desk and sat down. "I want you to call your gynecologist. Let him examine you and he'll be able to give you a better idea of the disease's effects."

"Can't you give me some idea? Will it hurt my baby?"

"Wait until your gynecologist examines you."

Joan was frightened when she returned home. Her mother waited in the living room.

"He told me I have rubella," Joan said as she hung up her coat and sat down opposite her mother. "He seemed concerned when I told him I might be pregnant again, but wouldn't tell me why. He said to see my gynecologist."

If Grandmother Kennedy understood, she kept it to herself. She had always provided silent and sturdy support to her daughter. The news made Joan feel even worse than before. "It's been a lousy two weeks, Mom." Her voice was weary.

"You'd better do what Dr. Rank suggests," Grandmother Kennedy said.

"I don't want to call. We don't need any more bad news this week." But she got up anyway. Maybe her gynecologist would be reassuring after all. She walked slowly to the kitchen, picked up the phone, and dialed. A nurse answered, and Joan asked for an appointment. She wasn't prepared for the response.

"I'm sorry, Mrs. Huber, the doctor says he can't see you until you're better."

"How long will that be?" Joan asked.

"About two weeks," the nurse said.

"Two weeks!"

"We can't take the chance that you might infect some of the other mothers in the office—many of them are pregnant."

All Joan could do was wait and hope that Dr. Rank's diagnosis was incorrect. But he was right. The entire Huber family came down with German measles.

Caring for the two sick children kept Joan busy for the next fourteen days and her mind off the measles. Christmas was less than three weeks away, and she had to prepare for the annual gathering of the McDonald-Huber clans. Grandmother Kennedy was over constantly. Besides, Joan was feeling much better and enjoyed the prospect of being pregnant again. She idealized a big, happy family.

Joan had always wanted four children when she and Dick were married in 1960. They met at the former Western Electric plant (now AT&T Technologies) in Allentown, where Joan had been a clerk-typist for several years after graduating from Allentown Central Catholic High School. Dick was several years older and had just returned to the company after military leave. They dated and it wasn't long before they were married, settling into a tiny second-floor apartment in Allentown. Michael was a harbinger of things to come. Soon there would be several little Hubers, and the family needed more room. Joan and Dick began looking for a small house, and the one on Troxell Street seemed the best bargain. It needed a great deal of work but offered the newlyweds a challenge. They took it eagerly.

Kathy was born in early 1963. Then came the rubella late in the year. Joan wasn't the only victim. Thousands of women across the country were infected with a disease that would have long-lasting effects on a future generation.

"Couldn't Dr. Rank tell you anything about the measles?" Dick asked Joan the evening after she had seen the doctor.

"He wouldn't."

"It's not that terrible, is it?" Dick asked. "I don't know," Joan said quietly.

Dick seldom revealed his emotions, but he showed his concern this time. Generally, he was steady and quiet, his deep voice reassuring to Joan. They complemented each other, Joan bubbly and Dick seemingly placid.

The early years ran through Joan's mind as she waited in the gynecologist's office two weeks later. She remembered the first time the doctor told her she was pregnant. She had smiled quietly, but inside was excited. She couldn't wait to call Dick. Those pleasant days were a buttress against the bad news she expected from the doctor. She kept her mind riveted on the past as she went into the examining room. It was empty, and she sat down to wait. When the doctor entered, he was matter-of-fact, almost abrupt.

"Has the rubella been confirmed, Joan?"

"Yes, my family doctor, Dr. Rank, diagnosed it."

"When was that?" the doctor asked.

"About two weeks ago."

"Let's find out whether you are pregnant," the doctor said. He moved quickly through the examination.

"You are," he said.

"What does that mean?"

"Joan, rubella can be a very destructive disease. There's a good chance your baby will be born handicapped. It could be heart problems, blindness, deafness, a combination of these defects or all of them."

Joan absorbed the words without feeling their impact.

7

Slowly, the ramifications of her illness that had seemed so mild, so innocent, burst upon her. She tried to visualize the tiny fetus being assaulted and what the child would look like in life.

"What are the chances my child will be born handicapped?"

The physician thought momentarily. "I'd say about fifty-fifty your baby will have some sort of defect."

"I guess I'll have to live with that," Joan said.

"You don't have to. I think an abortion would be the better part of wisdom. You can't have one in Pennsylvania, but the procedure is legal in New York City. I can set up an appointment at a hospital there."

Joan listened impatiently to the doctor, controlled and clinical in his white coat. She thought of her own children, Kathy, so plump and Germanic-looking, Michael, wiry and independent.

"I have two beautiful little kids at home. The thought of destroying something like that is entirely against my nature," Joan said, her voice strained.

"You want to have this baby, Joan. What about your husband? Does he want to have a child that could be handicapped?"

"He feels exactly the same way I do."

"How do you know?"

"I know."

It was more than her Catholicism that compelled Joan to fight for her child. The dictates of the church did have a powerful influence on her thinking. But Dick wasn't a Catholic and he believed in the sanctity of unborn life as strongly as Joan. Her natural instincts were to protect life wherever it was. She often said that society regarded life as cheap, to be disposed of like a throwaway bottle.

It was also Joan's fierce Irishness and loyalty to her family that aroused her ire. After all, she was part McDonald, and the struggles of her mother's family were her legacy. Had the McDonalds bowed to authority and power, the family would have been dispersed by well-meaning people. Grandma McDonald's strength and determination had held the clan together. She was in her early thirties in the first part of the century when her husband fell ill one night, and by morning was dead of spinal meningitis. Grandma McDonald struggled to survive, taking any work she could find, laboring during the day and leaving her brood of six children alone at home. Joan's mother was only ten and helped an older sister care for the children, the youngest of whom was two. The neighbors watched in horror as they roamed free during the day without adult supervision, and it wasn't long before welfare officials arrived on the doorstep. Grandma McDonald was sweeping the porch. She rested the broom and listened while they explained their mission. How could she raise a family of five children on her meager income? Someone suggested she give up her children and place them in foster homes. There was a sudden pause, then Grandma McDonald moved unexpectedly. With a screech she grabbed and raised her broom like a cudgel and charged. The startled bureaucrats scattered before the onslaught. Never would she allow it! Never! The family would manage better together than apart.

Joan looked at her gynecologist. "I'm not going to have an abortion. If you wish, I'll have my husband come to discuss it with you."

"I'd feel better about it if he did. There's not much time left to have a safe abortion."

Dick felt as Joan did. They would have their baby. If it was handicapped, that was God's will.

2

THE ROUTINE OF LIFE kept Joan going. The weeks blended into months, spring came, and she unpacked her old maternity clothes. Knowing it wouldn't make her pregnancy any easier, Joan refused to worry about the fate of her unborn baby and life with a handicapped child. She was too busy and exhausted most of the time to think about the future.

She could always turn to Grandmother Kennedy and Dick. Even Grandfather Kennedy was rooting for his Joanie, though he didn't like discussing unpleasant things. It was Grandmother Kennedy who would be at Joan's side on a moment's notice, to talk or sit for the children while Joan ran errands or kept appointments.

Joan's Irish-Catholicism also was a source of strength. She had learned as a child to accept life's vicissitudes. If something happened for the good, she thanked God. If it were for the worse, she accepted it. Joan was amused one day in confession when she told her priest that her doctor had recommended an abortion.

"By the way, Father, are there any special prayers for me?"

"You didn't have one, did you?" the priest demanded.

"Of course not," Joan said proudly. She awaited his praise.

"No," the priest said. "There are no special prayers for you."

Joan got a laugh from the way she looked, a full-bellied pregnant mom with Kathy on her hip and Mike darting about at her feet. Spring passed and Joan planned to have her baby under hypnosis. She had successfully delivered Mike and Kathy that way and the doctor was a pioneer in the use of this procedure during childbirth. His voice was deep, soothing, and calming to anxious mothers.

By August Joan was bulging. She kept moving, however, and on the fourth she and Dick took Grandmother, Grandfather, and the kids to a band concert in West Park, a small, manicured tract with tall trees and well-kept gardens. West Park was a throwback to another era without television, when people came out at night. The park's focal point was a permanent band shell surrounded by lawns, gardens, and trees, and the scene on a hot summer's evening recalled an Impressionist painting. Visitors lounged on the grass and in lawn chairs, listening to the music as the sun's rays filtered through the darkened, gently rustling leaves. Joan and Grandmother sat near the band with Kathy while Dick was off walking Mike. The band struck up the "Stars and Stripes Forever." It was appropriate for the evening, a rousing tune fit for the occasion. Suddenly Joan felt a stabbing pain in her abdomen.

"Oh, my gosh. You'd better get Dick," she cried. "I think I'm going into labor."

"Stay right here," Grandmother said. She dashed off

through the shaded dusk, startling Dick as she came toward him on the run.

"Joanie's not feeling well," Grandmother said out of breath. "I think we'd better go."

Dick grabbed Mike and they hurried back. By the time they got there, Joan had plunked Kathy in the stroller and was heading for the car. It was a mad drive home, through back streets, Joan anxiously awaiting each new episode of pain.

Joan went upstairs to lie down, and Grandmother followed while Grandfather lingered downstairs. The contractions subsided, and Grandmother and Grandfather went home after midnight.

"We may as well get some sleep. I expect it'll be a very busy day tomorrow," Grandmother said as she left Joan in bed. "Give me a call the minute you need me."

Dick took up the vigil dividing his time between Joan and Kathy, who was constantly awakened by the pain of cutting teeth. He went from room to room like a harried nurse, soothing first Kathy, then Joan.

By early morning the contractions were regular, coming five minutes apart. Dick decided it was time to get Joan to the hospital. He telephoned Grandmother Kennedy, but there was no answer.

"They must be dead to the world," he mumbled to Joan. "I'm going to go over and wake them."

Dick ran down to the old Ford and turned the ignition key. The engine spun fruitlessly. He looked at the gauges.

"I forgot to get gas!" he bellowed.

"What's the matter?" Joan called down from upstairs.

"The car's out of gas." Dick could hear Joan moaning softly.

He picked up the telephone and let it ring until Grandmother Kennedy answered. Her voice was groggy.

"It's Dick. I've got to get Joanie to the hospital. Can you get over here and watch the kids?"

"Be right there," Grandmother Kennedy said.

Joan heard a car stop outside and laughed when she saw her mother, disheveled and sleepy, with her dress inside out. She'd left the car in the middle of the street with the door wide open. It was comic relief that helped reduce the anxiety. This was the moment they both cherished and feared. Joan wondered how she would handle bad news. She ran through the possibilities: blindness, deafness, heart defects. Her eyes met her mother's.

"Now we'll know," Joan said quietly.

"Don't fret about it, Joanie. Let's just pray that everything will be OK."

Dick drove Joan down Union Boulevard into the city and out into the western suburbs where the Allentown Hospital rises seven stories above the nearby brick row houses. He pulled into the emergency room entrance and helped Joan out. She walked in and was seated in a wheelchair and taken to the fifth floor maternity area. Dawn was streaking the sky, and everything became a blur. The nurses chattered while patients labored. Doctors came and went, and Joan heard the voice of her own physician. He placed a thick hand on her arm and spoke quietly and forcefully. She could feel herself relax, the anxiety lessen. His deep voice seemed to penetrate to her soul. Then time seemed to stop.

Joan awoke, staring at the white ceiling of the delivery room. She tried to remember where she was, what day it was, the time. A wave of nausea overtook her, and she vomited. Suddenly she remembered. She'd had a baby. It all came back. She'd had rubella, the baby might be deformed or handicapped. This was the hospital. She remembered the labor room, being wheeled into the delivery room. She recalled the doctor's words. "Here comes the baby, just give us one more push." Then someone clamped a mask over her face. He hadn't relied on hypnosis. Why? What was wrong? As her head cleared, she was sure something had happened.

"The baby, where's my baby?" she cried.

"Joan. You have a little girl, and she's just fine, five pounds, four ounces."

"But how is she?" Joan asked.

"She's OK, Joan." The doctor's deep voice was reassuring. He motioned to a nurse, masked and dressed in white. She approached with Joan's baby, Mary Ellen Huber, lying on her belly along the nurse's palm and arm. "She is really fine," the doctor said. "I checked her heart. There's a slight murmur, but that's inconsequential. Her eyes are good, her lungs were full but that's been taken care of." He paused briefly. "She's small. But that's OK."

The effects of the gas lingered, robbing Joan of her chance to savor the birth of her child. She was moved from the fifth floor delivery room to the adjacent recovery area where she remained for several hours while Mary Ellen was taken downstairs to the nursery. Joan dozed, relaxed and contented. Her baby was well. "Thank God," she whispered to herself. "Thank God." When it was time to return to her room, a floor nurse appeared with a wheelchair.

"I understand you had a little girl," the nurse said.

Joan nodded, still groggy from the anesthetic.

"We'll go by the nursery and get a good look at her." It was a hospital tradition to show the mother her child. They stopped in the hall outside the nursery and Joan peered through the large plate-glass window at the rows of bassinets, all full. It seemed as if everyone was being born on August 5, 1964.

"We're here to see the Huber baby," the nurse said through the doorway into the nursery.

Joan could hear the nurses inside calling for her child. "Huber baby, Huber baby. Where's the Huber baby?"

"There's no Huber baby here," the floor nurse said.

"There has to be a Huber baby," said another. "This lady just had a baby."

Joan sat in the hallway listening as the nurses tried to find Mary Ellen. Fear mixed with the nausea. She slumped back, fighting the impression it was all a dream.

"Try the overflow nursery," a voice said. The floor nurse wheeled Joan up the hall. Again the request went out. "Huber baby, we're here to see the Huber baby." The nurses searched the bassinets and their records. Still, there was no Mary Ellen.

Joan fought for composure. "Something's happened to my baby. She wasn't OK. He just said that to me so I could recover." She fought the urge to become hysterical.

A nurse stepped into the hall.

"Are you Mrs. Huber? Don't worry, we'll find your baby."

Joan and the nurses laughed about the missing Huber baby the next day. Whenever a nurse entered her room on the fifth floor maternity ward, she pretended to look for the lost infant, under the bed, in the closet. Joan was amused by the acting. The search had ended happily when Mary Ellen was found in the isolation nursery, placed there as a precaution against the possibility she still carried the rubella virus. Dr. Rank was another visitor to Joan's room that day and he brought good news. He had examined Mary Ellen and found nothing to indicate the disease had harmed her.

"Mary Ellen seems to be a perfectly healthy little girl, Joan," Dr. Rank said.

"What about the murmur?" Joan asked.

"Nothing to worry about."

"The doctor said she was small," Joan said.

"Some babies are small. But she'll grow up to be a beautiful girl," he said smiling.

"There's nothing the matter with her?" Joan asked.

"Everything checks out except the hearing and we won't be able to test that properly until she's four or five."

"We're home free?" Joan asked.

"I sure hope so, Joan. But let's keep an eye on the hearing."

Deafness seemed like a minor handicap compared to what might have been. Joan knew that some deaf people used sign language and wore hearing aids. But that was all. Could they speak, learn language, mingle with others? She'd never thought about it. Why should she? She'd never known anyone who was deaf and she was sure now Mary Ellen would be a healthy child.

Nevertheless, Dr. Rank's warning made Joan restive. She asked Grandmother Kennedy to bring her as many articles about deafness as she could find. But little material was available and most of it dealt with how the deaf learn to communicate, using sign language and finger spelling.

There was another nagging doubt.

"I can't imagine waiting four years to see if Mary Ellen is deaf," Joan told her mother.

That didn't sit with Joan's character. She was bright and quick moving, "impatient" was the way she described herself. Joan believed it essential to determine the capabilities and extent of Mary Ellen's hearing as soon as possible, despite what Dr. Rank said.

But there seemed no need to worry the day Dick picked up Joan and Mary Ellen to take them home to Troxell Street. Joan was wheeled down to the emergency exit by a volunteer who helped her into the car. Dick got in the front seat and pulled the door shut. *Wham!* Mary Ellen jumped. Joan felt a surge of joy, and she and Dick exchanged glances. Mary Ellen did hear after all. They had just seen her respond.

3

THE KIDS WERE CURIOUS when Mary Ellen came home. They followed Joan, watching as she fed Mary Ellen, diapered and soothed her, and put her in for naps. Mike and Kathy peered into the bassinet, wide-eyed and questioning. Grandmother Kennedy was around the house more than usual, helping out, giving Joan time to rest.

During those first days, Joan watched her baby daughter carefully, waiting for some sign that she could not hear. But nothing indicated a problem. Mary Ellen acted and responded like any other newborn. She wailed when she was hungry or tired, took her bottle and ate well, and was aware that others were around. Joan was sure she would soon forget her fears. When Mary Ellen had her first checkup, Dr. Rank was unable to detect any anomaly. He assured Joan that Mary Ellen seemed like a perfectly normal child.

As the weeks passed, however, Joan sensed something different about Mary Ellen. A multitude of things encouraged her doubts, but they were so insignificant she couldn't relate specific concerns to Dr. Rank. Was it the way Mary Ellen looked or held her head, the way she cried, or the sound-ness of her sleep? Was Joan looking for something that didn't exist, like imagining an illness and then experiencing the symptoms? Dr. Rank smiled when she complained that Mary Ellen's sleep was different and that she had more of a screech than a voice. He counseled patience.

But Joan was an experienced mother and had a developed sense about what distinguishes a normal and abnormal child. Mike and Kathy were hardly beyond the infant stage, and Joan was familiar with the behavior and response of new-borns.

Joan also read voraciously on the subject of deafness. With every article, every book, her fears increased. Almost without exception, her readings told her that the critical years in the development of speech and language were from one to six, with the first year the most crucial. That squared with her own sense of logic.

Joan learned that children are exposed to words, even concepts, from birth, and babies learn to distinguish between various sounds. Language is something that develops and builds. Results aren't always immediately apparent. Why then were all the doctors saying otherwise?

"Joan, you're reading things into Mary Ellen's behavior," Dr. Rank said. "You've come through a difficult pregnancy and all your emotions are coming out now. Give Mary Ellen time. There's no way now to determine if she's deaf. Even if there were, there's nothing that can be done until she's older."

But the suspicions lingered as Joan left each appointment with Mary Ellen in her arms. The anxiety was pervasive. Even a good chat with Grandmother didn't always help. If she was distracted, it was only for a moment. She lived with butterflies in her stomach and her heart constantly skipped.

She was breathless whenever she climbed stairs and clutched Mary Ellen for fear of dropping her. She would pause and lean against the wall until the dizziness passed.

"Joanie, you don't look well. I think you should get more rest," Grandmother Kennedy said. Mike and Kathy played in the adjacent room and Mary Ellen fidgeted in her infant's seat.

"Oh, Mom, I'm so worried about Mary Ellen. She just doesn't seem right and I can't get anybody to agree with me. Dr. Rank thinks I'm overreacting. It's driving me crazy."

"You should get another opinion," Grandmother said. "You might stop worrying so much."

"It's not just the worrying, Mom. It's the kids. I never knew they required so much time. Look at Mike. He moves so much he'll never rust."

Grandmother Kennedy laughed. The trials of raising children took her back to when Joan and her brother, Eddie, were young.

"I remember," Grandmother said. "I know it's not easy. Look what you and Eddie did to me. Turned my hair white."

Grandmother touched the snow-white, curly hair that was wound in a French twist. It had been black as anthracite when she was a young woman.

Joan laughed. She could always laugh, even in the worst of times. It was part of that Kennedy stoicism.

Together Joan and Grandmother Kennedy watched Mary Ellen, their maternal instincts sharpened by weeks of observation. One trait that seemed subtle and inconsequential at first began intruding on Joan. As newborns, all the Huber babies slept in Joan and Dick's bedroom. Joan liked it that way. She could reach over and pick up Mary Ellen or feed her in the middle of the night. When Mike was the only child, maintaining quiet during nap time was no problem.

But when Kathy came along, Mike was kept away from the room. When Mary Ellen was born, he played cowboys and Indians throughout the house and Kathy was his sidekick. The new baby was the center of mom's attention, and Mike certainly had to be there when Joan and Mary Ellen were together. He would come bounding up the stairs with his cap pistol blasting.

"Shhh," Joan warned when Mary Ellen took her afternoon nap. "The baby is sleeping."

Mike stopped and peered in at his new sister. Soon he forgot or ignored his mother's scolding and jabbered away in the bedroom, only to be silenced again. At first Joan didn't notice the difference between Mary Ellen's behavior and that of Mike and Kathy when they were the same age. She was too busy keeping them quiet upstairs. It dawned on her though that Mary Ellen was a sound sleeper. The cavortings and crashings of her brother and sister didn't seem to bother her.

Joan dismissed her new suspicion. "You really are reading things into this," she said to herself. Nevertheless, she was afraid. She tried to rationalize it away, but it wouldn't go. Even medical opinions seemed so superficial that Joan hardly believed doctors could offer them. She took Mary Ellen to one specialist who said that, like many babies, Mary Ellen was "sophisticated to sound." She heard normally, he assured Joan, and added that in an infant's world there were so many sights and sounds, so many visual and auditory distractions, that Mary Ellen just couldn't respond to isolated and individual sounds. An infant could be seated next to a dog when it barked and be unaware that the sound came from the animal. Children eventually learned that all sounds have origins and they must learn the source. It doesn't come naturally, he said.

21

Joan's scoldings in the bedroom became less frequent. Without realizing it, she relaxed her discipline because Mary Ellen could sleep through the commotion. Joan assured herself that Mary Ellen's sleep patterns were different. The rest of the day she seemed perfectly normal; she wriggled just like any baby and was alert. Mike and Kathy played and watched television in the playroom next to the kitchen while Mary Ellen was with Joan. Her eyes followed everything. Her little arms were constantly in motion, and she giggled when Joan tickled and caressed her.

Grandmother and Grandfather Kennedy sometimes visited after dinner, and they all gathered in the living room to rock the baby and read to the children before bedtime. These were moments Joan cherished. She was off her feet, the day's work was done. She held Mary Ellen in her lap and gently rocked her to sleep. Dick took a turn, as did Grandmother and Grandfather Kennedy. Grandfather Kennedy was a heavy smoker and had developed a severe, wracking cough that startled the children. When Mike was an infant, Grandfather's cough jolted him out of a slumber and Joan ruled that Grandfather had to cough in the kitchen. As Mike and Kathy grew older, the rule was relaxed and occasionally Grandfather Kennedy's cough filled the room. Mary Ellen was several months old when Grandmother and Grandfather visited one night in the fall of 1964. The family gathered in the living room, and Joan held Mary Ellen in the rocker. Suddenly Grandfather coughed, deep and rasping. Joan tried to shield her dozing daughter, but Mary Ellen remained in a deep sleep on Joan's lap.

"Did you notice Mary Ellen's reaction to Dad's cough?" Joan asked Grandmother Kennedy.

"No. Why? Did she startle?"

"Mike and Kathy would have jumped through the roof," Joan said. "Mary Ellen didn't budge."

Joan realized also that Grandmother and Grandfather no longer whispered around Mary Ellen when she was in her crib. They weren't aware of the change, but Joan was. She'd been watching and was beginning to accept the reality that her youngest daughter didn't hear well—or hear at all.

Joan had to find out the truth, once and for all. Otherwise the anxiety would go on for years, which was a more depressing prospect than facing the facts. The big plastic jewelry box in her bedroom would be a good test; that would make enough noise to startle anyone if dropped on the floor. Joan decided to do it when Mary Ellen took her afternoon nap. She crept down the hall, the box in her hands. Her palms were moist and she could feel her heart beating rapidly. She paused in the doorway, then carried the box over to the crib.

"Oh, pray to God she'll wake up," Joan whispered. She held the box waist high, then let it go. The crash was like a loud gunshot. Joan stood motionless, her eyes wide with expectation and hope. Mary Ellen was so peaceful, her tiny hand held to her mouth, her eyes closed, and the light brown hair falling gently over her forehead. Her breathing came evenly and quietly. She was still asleep.

4

"SOMEBODY'S GOT TO BELIEVE ME!"

"Give her more time, Joan," Dr. Rank said. His tone was pleading.

"But I'm sure she can't hear!"

"She's only a couple of months old, Joan. There's no way we can tell until she's older."

Joan listened dutifully as she carried Mary Ellen, bundled against the winter, back and forth to his office. It was impossible to know whether Mary Ellen was deaf. She played well with Mike and Kathy, was aggressive and progressing through most of the infant stages. She sat up when she was supposed to, smiled and gurgled and began to crawl early. She was as demanding as the others when they were her age and was becoming a nuisance to her brother and sister, always getting into things, screeching in a strange voice. She was alert and her eyes followed Joan's everywhere.

Dick wouldn't have noticed a problem had it not been for Joan's concern. He was off early in the morning to his job as benefits representative at Western Electric and didn't get home until five. The scene he saw when he walked through the door was typical of any American household with three small children. The kids rushed from the playroom shrieking their greetings, Mike in the lead, Kathy falling and stumbling as she learned to walk, and Mary Ellen right behind, crawling. Dick and Joan hardly had time to say hello to each other.

Dick observed Mary Ellen carefully each evening.

"She seems so normal," he said after the kids had been put to bed.

"That's the problem," Joan said. "She does the things infants are supposed to do. So how do you convince the doctor there's something wrong just because she has a strange voice and is a sound sleeper?"

Joan also was troubled because Mary Ellen didn't babble. Any infant her age should be developing basic speech patterns, and Joan knew from her reading that babbling is an important step in language development. It represented an infant's first experiments with sounds and speech. Joan remembered the hours of gentle cooing and babble from Mike and Kathy, their playing with sounds and syllables, sometimes expressed at the top of their lungs. Mary Ellen's utterances, on the other hand, were piercing screams that annoyed and frightened Joan. They weren't normal. Mary Ellen would sit in her high chair, her little arms and legs wriggling, and screech like a banshee.

Instinctively Joan held her daughter and spoke into her ear, trying to instill words and language. There was growing desperation in Joan's attempts. She wanted Mary Ellen to babble and coo like any normal infant. When Joan changed her diaper, she would nestle her nose into Mary Ellen's ear and speak gently: "Mama, *m–a–a–m–a–a, m–a–a–m–a–a,*" Joan would repeat. "Mama, *m–a–a–m–a–a.*"

"I hate to harp," Joan told Dr. Rank in the familiar surroundings of his office, "but I've been doing some testing and I'm not sure that Mary Ellen hears anything." Dr. Rank listened while they stood next to the examining table where Mary Ellen lay stripped to her diaper. The complaint was familiar, but this time Joan's insistence was more compelling. Her face was tense and he sympathized with her anguish. Mary Ellen's condition hadn't improved, or at least Joan said it hadn't.

"What kind of testing, Joan?" Dr. Rank asked.

"She doesn't rouse from sleep no matter how much noise, and that was never the case with my other two. I know it sounds ridiculous, but both Kathy and Mike would wake up when my father coughed. He has a terrible smoker's cough, but it doesn't bother Mary Ellen at all. She also doesn't babble the way infants are supposed to, and the only way she seems to communicate verbally is by screaming."

Dr. Rank could no longer dismiss Joan's fears. "Put her up in this baby chair and face her away from us," he said.

Joan lifted Mary Ellen into the seat and turned her toward the wall of the examining room. Dr. Rank stood directly behind Mary Ellen and clapped his hands. There was no response. He clapped again and again from the right, then the left, from above and below. Nothing happened. Mary Ellen seemed oblivious to the noise, and continued playing with her feet. Dr. Rank was perplexed.

"I don't know," he said. "It looks like there may be a problem." He was pensive for a moment. "Sometimes you just can't tell. But Mary Ellen should be old enough to hear that clapping." He pulled out a pad and pencil. "I'm going to refer you to the State Department of Health. They have a mobile team of therapists who will test Mary Ellen in less than an hour. I'll set up an appointment and let you know when they're in town."

For Joan, the continuing uncertainty was like being in purgatory. She needed to know if her baby daughter was deaf, but she still didn't fully comprehend the problems of deafness. If Mary Ellen were deaf, would she learn to speak and acquire language skills? Joan thought she could. But if so, why were there schools for the deaf where students communicated with balletlike gestures of the hands and body? It was terrifying to think of Mary Ellen winding up among students whose speech was distorted, nasal, and incomprehensible, their sign language understood only by those who had mastered it. For the most part, sign language was the only method of communication in those schools and little emphasis was placed on acquiring speech and language. Most teachers of the deaf refused to believe it possible for the deaf to speak normally, much less hear, and spent little time teaching sounds, syllables, words, sentences—the necessary components of the spoken language. What if her efforts to teach Mary Ellen to speak, heroic though they were, were futile?

Sometimes the health department therapists came to Allentown only twice a year. As the wait stretched out, Joan's anxiety increased. If she bent over to pick up a toy or tie a shoelace, she was staggered when she stood upright as the blood rushed from her head.

"Joanie, you're worrying me again," Grandmother Kennedy said while she and Joan sipped coffee at Grandmother's house. Dick had the children this Saturday morning and Joan enjoyed being alone. There were no chores to do, no mouths to feed, and she marveled at how clean Grandmother kept everything. What a contrast to

Troxell Street. No wonder Grandmother's nickname was Dutch Cleanser.

"I know, Mom. I'm planning to see Dr. Rank about it. I've been getting dizzy and I think it's from low blood pressure."

"Make sure you see him," Grandmother Kennedy urged.

Joan was becoming accustomed to getting medical attention for herself whenever she took the children to Dr. Rank. She would have ignored the dizziness but was afraid of fainting around the children.

"I want you to take my blood pressure," she told Dr. Rank on a visit to his office with Mary Ellen.

"Why?"

"I think it's low. When I go upstairs carrying Mary Ellen, I'm afraid I'm going to faint."

Dr. Rank reached for the sphygmomanometer. "I doubt very much, Joan, that your blood pressure is the problem." He wrapped the cuff around her arm and began pumping. "You're emotionally exhausted and the anxiety is manifesting itself through these spells. It's common." He concentrated on his watch for a moment. "You're fine." He returned the blood pressure gauge to its drawer. "I'm going to recommend that you get out of the house at least once a week. Get completely away from your family, take a break. Call up a girlfriend or your mother and go to the movies, go bowling. Do anything. Just get away from the house and the kids. You're dwelling far too much on Mary Ellen."

"But I can handle it!" Joan protested. She was almost more stunned than when she learned she had rubella; insulted too. Her family depended on her, and Dr. Rank was suggesting that she was incapable of doing her job.

She told Dick that she'd been ordered out of the house once a week. What could she do? Going to the movies or bowling wasn't appealing. That was just passing time.

"You like going out with your mother," Dick said.

"We're doing that more often now," Joan replied. She and Grandmother Kennedy occasionally went to a nearby restaurant where Joan had her favorite, a big, juicy pizzaburger. It was becoming a regular outing now that Mary Ellen was more demanding. Dick came home and Joan went out with Grandmother, sometimes on the spur of the moment. Joan and Dick established a code when Joan had had enough.

"I've got cabin fever," she would say as Dick came into the kitchen after work.

Finally, Joan decided that art classes would be an excellent diversion. She had had a natural talent for painting in high school, but when the kids came along she no longer had time. The Allentown school district was offering an art course across town at one of the high schools and Joan decided to sign up. She loved holding her brushes, the smell of oils, and the feel of charcoal. Joan also enjoyed the company. The class was filled with women like herself who wished to rekindle an interest they had dropped because of family responsibilities.

"Hello, Joan. How have you been?"

Joan regarded the woman quizzically, trying to recall where they had met. The voice and features were familiar, but she couldn't place them.

"Mildred Kovacs. Remember? Western Electric?"

A smile broke over Joan's face. They had been co-workers at Western Electric and shared many coffee breaks. Both had married and started raising children. But while Joan's first two children were healthy, Mildred's little girl hadn't been. Shortly after birth something went awry and doctors diagnosed the resulting brain damage as an allergic reaction to medication. The child was left severely handicapped, unable to feed herself or even sit up. Mildred performed virtually every function for her daughter, and Joan was impressed by Mildred's ability to laugh through her adversity.

"I think we're kindred spirts," Joan told her mother. "Mildred has a baby girl who is badly handicapped, yet Mildred moves through life with such ease. And Mary Ellen is so healthy. I mean even if she turns out to be deaf, it would be nothing compared to what Mildred is going through."

Joan and Mildred lived near each other and began commuting to class together. They laughed all the way to downtown Allentown, and were still giggling as they walked into class, always late.

"For once I'd like to see you two before I hear you coming down the hall," the teacher quipped good-naturedly.

Joan threw herself into her painting, and one by one her landscapes began going up on the walls around the house. Dr. Rank's suggested therapy was working. The attacks of dizziness subsided, and Joan's body was returning to normal. She realized how much she owed to Mildred and the way she accepted life without anger or remorse. Joan dropped by her house one night to meet Mildred's daughter, and as she and Joan talked, Mildred cradled the child, talking to her constantly, treating her as though she were perfectly normal.

"How do you do it?" Joan asked. "You're so great with your little girl."

Mildred smiled. "It's funny about children. Before she was born, I was afraid of having a handicapped child. I used to think how devastating it would be for anyone. When it happened to me, I realized there was no one else in the world to help this child. I was the only one. She needs as much love as any other child and she's mine. I'll always love her, no matter what."

"My Mary Ellen may be deaf, and it upsets me so much," Joan said quietly. "Then I see you with your child, and I realize I can handle deafness."

"How do you know she's deaf?" Mildred asked.

"Just suspicions. I had rubella when I was carrying her and she's normal. But we haven't checked her hearing yet. I keep taking her to the doctor and he says she's too young to test."

"Nothing is ever as bad as it seems," Mildred said.

The course ended, and Joan and Mildred drifted apart. But Joan never forgot. "God put Mildred in my path," she told Grandmother Kennedy. "Our meeting was no coincidence. He was telling me that before I start feeling sorry for myself He would show me what strength was all about and how lucky I really am."

Her friendship with Mildred gave Joan renewed courage, and she continued prompting Mary Ellen, talking to her, teaching her words. But it didn't seem to do any good.

"*Ma, Ma, Maa, Maa,*" Joan kept repeating. The response was always the same. If Mary Ellen was in her crib, she would roll around and scream—a high-pitched, unnatural noise, as though she couldn't hear to imitate the sounds in her environment. Joan continued to read about speech and language development, growing more alarmed as Mary Ellen missed these critical days. Yet no one seemed concerned. No one offered advice except to counsel patience, and Joan was running out of that. Where could she go? To whom could she turn? Joan was finding that the experts were ignorant and really didn't understand the ramifications of deafness. They just assumed any deaf child would acquire sign language and carry on.

5

THE MONTHS OF DOUBT and anxiety were a test of their young marriage, but Joan and Dick were drawn closer together. Joan relied on Dick's calming presence and his ability to listen. She admired him for his serenity, knowing the demands of his job. He attended to his family's needs first after work, helping Joan whenever he could, sharing her highs and lows and struggling with the problem of Mary Ellen. He had learned to cope with stress, or at least not to show it. Like Joan, he accepted life as it came. His father had died of a heart attack when he was two, and his mother had worked and left Dick in the care of a neighbor who became a surrogate mother. From an early age, Dick learned the necessity of self-reliance and independence, and Joan always attributed his quiet maturity to those youthful experiences.

That was past life. In the present, the Hubers' baby daughter might be handicapped, but she was blossoming into a beautiful child. Like Mike, she was acquiring more of Joan's features, while Kathy was more like her father. Mary Ellen was tiny, small-boned, with blond curly hair and blue eyes.

But while little girls are expected to be quiet, mannerly, and well-behaved, Mary Ellen was anything but. She was a budding cutup and was dubbed "the hell-machine" whenever she was in her walker. She moved it around the downstairs at breakneck speed, crashing into furniture, annoying her siblings, forcing Joan to keep a watch on her at all times. When she was not in the walker, one of her favorite tricks was to unscrew the screen from the kitchen storm door. Until she was discovered, it appeared that she was gazing pensively out the kitchen door. But with her tiny delicate hands, she was removing the screws that held the screen in place. When someone hurriedly went through the door, the screen would come tumbling out.

Summer was drawing to a close when Joan finally received word that two staffers from the state health department would be in the Allentown area. The news was unsettling. This was the first time Mary Ellen would be tested by professionals who could tell whether she was deaf. Joan was restless the day she took Mary Ellen to a nearby hospital where the team was to perform the tests. They walked down the steps into a long basement hallway, Joan anxious about the impending examination, Mary Ellen oblivious to her mother's nervousness. As usual, she was alert, curious, and noisy. Joan tried to restrain her, but Mary Ellen paid no attention. She popped up again to resume her adventures in the hallway. The experience of waiting reminded Joan of labor. She wondered how she would react if told Mary Ellen was deaf. What would they say, what kind of treatment would they suggest? Would Mary Ellen have to go to special schools? Joan was hoping she was another hysterical mother who dreamed up imagined maladies to explain her daughter's behavior. She wanted the women to turn to her and say, "Mrs. Huber, there's nothing wrong with

David Colley

your daughter. It's just . . ." Joan's thoughts trailed off. She
was aware of the sights, sounds, and smells of the hospital.
The hallway was busy, filled with patients, doctors, and
nurses, people dressed as though they belonged in the hospital, others who wore street clothes.

"Mrs. Huber. You may bring Mary Ellen in now."

Joan looked up. A woman stood in the doorway of the
room where Mary Ellen was to be tested. She was plain-
looking and reminded Joan of a schoolteacher. She smiled
and introduced herself and her associate as Joan led Mary
Ellen into the room. The walls were of beige-colored tile. A
desk was positioned on the far side, and several chairs were
arranged around it. A table was pulled out into the middle
with a chair on either side. Mary Ellen sat on Joan's lap as
the woman explained the test. Mary Ellen would sit on the
table while one therapist made sounds from behind. The
other would observe Mary Ellen from the front.

Joan placed Mary Ellen on the table and sat in a corner as
the two women took up their positions, one in front with a
note pad, the other behind with gadgets and noisemakers.
The tester reached into a box, retrieved a bell, and rang it
behind Mary Ellen's head. There was no response. Joan
watched Mary Ellen's expression. She could see the devices
being rattled behind her daughter's back. The woman with
the writing pad jotted down notes. The tester rang the bell
in a wide circle around Mary Ellen's head. She took other
noisemakers and moved them high and low, to the left, to
the right. They clicked, honked, and buzzed. Joan's anxiety
increased as the woman in front continued to take notes.
The two therapists seemed puzzled by the lack of response,
but said nothing.

The tester reached into her box and pulled out a cellophane cigarette wrapper with the red pull-string still at-

34

tached. She crumbled it in her fingers and held it out, almost against Mary Ellen's right ear. The crumbling made a crisp sound, like a crackling fire. Suddenly, Mary Ellen turned her head toward the sound. Joan watched transfixed.

"She heard that," the therapist said.

Joan was puzzled. Mary Ellen had never responded to anything before with that ear. Why this time? She was certain she'd seen the woman's hand brush against Mary Ellen's dangling curls.

"Are you sure?" Joan asked.

"Yes, she heard it."

These were the words Joan wanted to hear, and it was the first time that anyone said that Mary Ellen had heard sound. Joan felt her body relax as though she had swallowed a tranquilizer. She dismissed the need to explain why Mary Ellen hadn't heard the first sounds. She'd find out in due course. For now, the women from the health department were satisfied that Mary Ellen wasn't deaf. There was a slight problem and a complete diagnosis was lacking.

"We'd like to see your daughter in another six months. We'll do another test, and maybe things will be even more promising at that time," the woman said to Joan. "For now, I think you can rest assured that Mary Ellen did hear something."

Joan drove the few miles home caught between rising elation and dread. Hadn't she seen the tester's hand brush against Mary Ellen's hair? But the woman seemed so certain and had not diagnosed Mary Ellen as deaf. Joan was willing to wait another six months. There was time in those months, time in which Mary Ellen might change. Most of all, there was hope.

The next six months went quickly. The children demanded most of Joan's attention. Mike, Kathy, and Mary

35

Ellen spent much of their time in the playroom adjacent to the kitchen where they had their toys and the television, which played constantly. Amid the noise and confusion, Grandmother Kennedy's daily visits were a relief to Joan, and the two sat at the kitchen table as chaos reigned around them. By the end of the day Joan longed to sit quietly and rock the children or read to them before bedtime. She vacillated between hope and despair. She wanted to believe the state therapists, but Mary Ellen wasn't progressing. The television was a nagging clue. Mike and Kathy were always glued to the set, watching cartoons and children's programs, but Mary Ellen never showed interest. She was off in her own little play world or pestering her brother and sister. She would harass and test them until Mike or Kathy retaliated and Mary Ellen would come running to Mama in the kitchen.

She was so happy and active. Why couldn't she show more progress in her speech and hearing, Joan wondered, and she began extending her efforts to force Mary Ellen to speak.

"Mama, *m–a–a–m–a–a,*" Joan repeated constantly. When Mary Ellen came into the kitchen to escape the wrath of her siblings, Joan used the opportunity to work with her, speaking forcefully, hoping Mary Ellen would hear. It was so frustrating. "*M–a–a–m–a–a.*" Mary Ellen was oblivious. Slowly, though, Joan began seeing slight progress. Mary Ellen seemed to be trying to mimic her mother.

"*Maw,*" was the faint reply. It was imperceptible at first. The word seemed to form in Mary Ellen's mind over a period of weeks.

"Something *is* there," Joan kept saying to herself. The state people were right after all. Maybe with work, Mary Ellen would snap out of whatever it was that was holding her back. Joan continued her instruction program with renewed determination. If Mary Ellen could be taught to say Mama, she could be taught the entire language. Why not? No one had said it couldn't be done.

"Bye-bye. Bye-bye," Joan repeated to Mary Ellen. Friends and relatives would leave the house, and Joan would show Mary Ellen how to wave and mouth the words, "bye-bye." She kept at it for weeks, and finally Mary Ellen began to respond. "Bye, bye. Bye, bye." It didn't sound quite like the real thing, but it was close enough. It was the ray of hope that Joan needed.

"I think she's saying bye-bye," Joan told Grandmother Kennedy one day.

Grandmother watched as Joan formed the words with her mouth and spoke them slowly.

"Bye-bye. Bye-bye."

Mary Ellen responded with a mumbled phrase. "See!" Joan cried out.

"Sounds like it could be," Grandmother said. She too formed the words and slowly spoke them to Mary Ellen.

Winter passed and summer was well entrenched when the health department informed Joan its therapists were returning to Allentown. Mary Ellen was almost two and making some progress, but it was slow. If they diagnosed her as deaf, what would that mean? Joan tried to put it out of her mind as she and Mary Ellen made the trip back to the hospital. They sat in the crowded hallway until the same two women greeted them. They sat Mary Ellen on the table and took up their positions in front and back. The woman behind began making noises with the various gadgets. Joan watched from the corner as the sounds were made around Mary Ellen's head. She wanted to cry. There was no response, even to the crinkling of cellophane. The two women were businesslike, but their faces registered concern.

"Mrs. Huber," one woman began after the test was over. "It appears as though Mary Ellen is not hearing all these sounds."

It was nothing new to Joan. Still, it was wrenching when someone else finally suggested that Mary Ellen might be deaf. She awaited their verdict and recommendations like a prisoner expecting the death sentence.

"We certainly recommend that you take Mary Ellen to an ear, nose, and throat specialist. He will analyze the problem."

Another doctor! Still, the lingering uncertainty seemed more comfortable than the prospect of knowing that Mary Ellen was deaf. Maybe if she worked with Mary Ellen long enough, the problem would go away. She struggled with Mary Ellen in her high chair, when she changed diapers, when Mary Ellen was on the potty, when Mary Ellen came to her for help.

"Mama, *m–a–a–m–a–a*," Joan kept saying. Grandmother Kennedy watched her daughter working with Mary Ellen and hid her own tears and sorrow. Grandmother offered comfort when she could. But it was obvious that Mary Ellen needed a specialist. Reluctantly Joan called for an appointment.

Grandfather Kennedy drove Joan and Mary Ellen to the ear, nose, and throat specialist several weeks later while Grandmother sat with Mike and Kathy. He wouldn't dwell on Mary Ellen and preferred not to hear of Joan's problems. It was too painful. She had always been special and he still insisted on showing her baby pictures to anyone who would look. In his mid-fifties, he had gained a few pounds and was not the same slender, black-haired Irishman he had been at forty. As he grew more stout and white, Joan's friends said he resembled Spencer Tracy.

Joan could feel the constriction in her stomach as her father chatted aimlessly. He pulled up to the front entrance, and dropped them off. Joan took Mary Ellen into the waiting room, trying to remain calm and hide the fears from the others in the room. A nurse called her name, and she carried Mary Ellen into the examining room to wait for the doctor.

"Hello, Mrs. Huber," the doctor said as he opened the door. "This must be Mary Ellen." Joan would not forget his features and demeanor. He was the person who could destroy the tranquillity of her life with a few words. He was a brusque man of medium height, though the white physician's coat made him appear taller. Joan noticed that his hairline was receding and that his countenance was rather stern. He wasted little time and asked for a short history of Mary Ellen's problem. He listened impatiently as Joan spoke, then picked up a tuning fork from a set on a counter.

"Put Mary Ellen on this table and face her away from us."

Joan complied. The doctor struck a tuning fork with an abrupt smack on the palm of his hand, setting off singing vibrations. He placed it close behind the left ear, then behind the right ear. Smack—ping. Smack—ping. Joan would always remember the sound. He picked up another fork. Smack—ping. Smack—ping. There was no expression on his face, and Joan could not read his thoughts. It was as though he were a mechanic working on an engine. Joan stood beside him as the test continued. Finally he put down the last tuning fork, frowned a bit, and turned to her.

"Mrs. Huber," he said in a voice that was almost scolding, "your daughter is profoundly deaf."

Had he hit her in the face with his fist, the blow could not have been harder. She gasped for breath and words. Suddenly it was over. The diagnosis seemed so logical. Why had it taken so long? She fought to regain her composure.

"You mean she'll have a speech impediment?" Joan asked.

The doctor looked at Joan as though weighing the impact of his words.

"Impediment?" he questioned sharply. "You'll be lucky if your daughter ever talks!"

"You mean she'll have no language at all?"

The doctor shook his head.

"But she has learned to say a few words," Joan said, pleading with him to offer hope.

"There may be some hearing there, but very little. I'm sorry, Mrs. Huber, but there's really nothing that can be done for Mary Ellen. I think it advisable for you to take her to Philadelphia. One of the major hospitals there can evaluate her and determine the extent of deafness. I'll have my secretary make an appointment for you as you leave."

The doctor turned and walked from the room. Joan was barely hanging on. She wanted to flee with her daughter in her arms, flee from this tragedy. Why couldn't this doctor offer more help? He was so cold and unfeeling. Joan gathered herself and Mary Ellen and walked back into the waiting room. The eyes of patients followed her over to the reception desk as she struggled to keep from becoming hysterical. The receptionist seemed part of the terrible conspiracy, so matter-of-fact and pleasantly unfeeling. Joan wanted her father to pick her up immediately and take her home. She wanted to go back to being a child, to forget the cares of the world, to have her mother and father taking care of *her*. She asked for the phone.

"While you're calling for a ride, I'll make an appointment for you in Philadelphia."

Joan's mother answered at home.

"How are you?" she asked.

"Not so good," Joan replied quietly, her voice shaking. "Please tell Pops to come pick me up. We're finished. Please hurry."

It seemed like hours before Grandfather Kennedy rolled into the parking lot and Joan and Mary Ellen got in. He had heard the bad news but kept the conversation light, winking at Mary Ellen as he drove them home. Mary Ellen responded to Grandfather Kennedy, but Joan could only stare out the window. She was heartbroken, yet puzzled. What did this all mean? She had none of the answers, and no one was providing them.

Grandfather Kennedy pulled into Troxell Street, parked the car in the driveway, and helped Joan and Mary Ellen out. Old friends of the Kennedys had stopped by for a visit, and Joan stiffened her lip and greeted them before excusing herself.

"I'll look after the children," Grandmother said. "You run upstairs and rest."

Joan climbed the stairs to the bedroom and burst into tears as she fell on the bed. Grandmother wasn't far behind.

"Joanie, what happened?"

Joan looked up. She hadn't heard her mother enter the room and was aware of Grandmother's presence only when she sat on the edge of the bed.

"Oh, Mom . . ." Joan's words became sobs as she rose and rested her head on Grandmother's shoulder. "He said Mary Ellen is profoundly deaf."

Grandmother held her daughter and patted her gently on the back. They didn't speak for several minutes as Joan sobbed. Joan pulled herself away and wiped at the tears.

"At least we know what the problem is now," Grandmother said.

"But she was doing so well," Joan said. "She was actually learning a few words. The doctor said she'll probably never speak."

"The doctor isn't God," Grandmother Kennedy replied softly.

"He thought he was," Joan snapped. "He told me to take her to Philadelphia for an evaluation. I'm getting so tired of doctors."

"When?" Grandmother asked.

"In two weeks." Joan started to get up.

"Have faith, Joanie. The Lord knows better than we do. Now just lie down and rest."

"I can't."

"Why not?" Grandmother asked.

"I've got to make dinner."

6

THE RICH GREEN PENNSYLVANIA countryside had turned various shades of orange and red when Joan, Dick, and Mary Ellen drove the fifty miles from Allentown to Philadelphia to keep an appointment at the medical college hearing clinic. Dick headed south on the Pennsylvania Turnpike Extension while Joan distracted Mary Ellen, who never traveled well after the first few minutes. The highway cuts through rich farmland, then through macadamized suburbs before ending in the outskirts of Philadelphia. Dick struggled through the increasing traffic, toward center city, through blocks of red brick row houses. The massive complex of the medical college loomed ahead as they parked and walked into an annex adjacent to the main buildings where Mary Ellen would undergo a complete evaluation to determine the extent of her hearing loss. There would be no guesswork this time, no simple tests with tuning forks or cellophane. The examination would be thorough, the diagnosis final, and Joan was resigned to the outcome. She knew what the results would be and was almost thankful that the years of doubt would be over. Now it was just a matter of determining the severity of Mary Ellen's handicap.

The doctors and audiologists were young and performed with a relaxed professionalism. They bombarded Joan with preliminary questions before Mary Ellen received the main test, a hearing examination conducted in a soundproof booth. An audiologist explained the procedure. Joan and Mary Ellen would be placed in the small enclosure and subjected to various pitches of sound. If Mary Ellen heard one, she was to push a button that activated several small mechanical animals in front of her. Joan tried to explain to Mary Ellen what she was to do and they took their places. But Mary Ellen would not sit still. Joan sat her down. She popped back up, grabbing the mechanical animals and pulling off their heads.

"That's not what we're here for," Joan admonished.

Mary Ellen persisted. She was up again, dismantling another animal. Finally, Joan got her seated, and the test began. The sounds came, low and throaty tones that seemed as though they came from a softly played harmonica, and shrill, high-pitched sounds like a natural ringing in the ears. Joan listened and watched. Mary Ellen fidgeted in her chair and gazed about, unaware of the sound.

All of their preparation didn't keep the final diagnosis from striking deep within Joan and Dick. The doctors tried to break the news as gently as possible: Mary Ellen was profoundly deaf. The clinic staff had thoroughly checked the hearing in both ears and found the left side better than the right, which the specialists said was so "dead" that no amount of training would ever bring it back.

What could they do? This was the middle of the twentieth century, the space age. Surely something could be done. But the doctors were glum. There was little they could offer for someone as deaf as Mary Ellen. They regarded Joan sadly when she asked how long it would take Mary Ellen to learn to speak. They explained the diagnosis as clearly as possible. The rubella had damaged the nerves that carried signals from the inner ear to the hearing center in the brain.

The doctors were specific. There was no hope for Mary Ellen. She would not speak, ever. She was enclosed in a world of silence. It would always be that way.

Joan and Dick reviewed their thoughts alone as they drove north to Allentown. Seated between them, Mary Ellen jabbered her nonsense language. The news was terrible, but Joan rallied on the way home. She would be her teacher, Mary Ellen's Annie Sullivan. Joan thought of Helen Keller, who had broken out of her world of silence because of the persistence of her teacher. Mary Ellen was able to say several words, and it was just a matter of time before she learned more. Besides, the people at the hearing clinic had recommended that Mary Ellen be fitted with a powerful hearing aid and start therapy. That gave Joan a boost.

"If she's learning words with nothing, just think of what I can get her to do with hearing aids," Joan thought. There was no telling what could be accomplished. Mary Ellen would put on hearing aids and that would be that. She would hear just like anyone else, maybe not quite as well, but she'd acquire speech and language and live normally. "That's not tough to take," Joan thought.

Joan immediately called a hearing-aid dealer who appeared on the Hubers' doorstep soon after their return from Philadelphia. Before Mary Ellen could wear her aid, though, he had to take impressions to insure a proper fit of the ear molds. That was a simple enough procedure for an adult, but for Mary Ellen it meant that Joan had to hold her down. She screamed and kicked while the impressions were made, and it seemed to take hours before the plasterlike material hardened. When the dealer returned a week later, Mary Ellen was just as hostile, though initially she wore the molds without reaction. She would fight back later.

Joan soon learned some of the side effects caused by hearing aids. Ear molds irritated Mary Ellen's skin, and it took months to accustom her to the chafing and soreness. Callouses had to develop in her ears before she could wear them comfortably, and her ears often bled before the skin hardened. It would be a year or more before she accepted them as an extension of herself and stopped trying to pull them out. It was a contest that Joan knew she had to win, and there were frequent skirmishes. Joan and Dick returned home one evening from a night out and found Grandmother crying hysterically. Mary Ellen had pulled out her molds and flushed them down the toilet before Grandmother could retrieve them. On another occasion she buried them in her sandbox and Joan spent hours trying to find them. With deliberate calculation, Mary Ellen had hidden them in a rusty can used for scooping sand. She bit another pair in two. Ear molds were expensive and had to be changed at regular intervals because, as Mary Ellen grew, they no longer fit snugly. Loose ear molds caused acoustic feedback and whistling hearing aids.

The state recommended a single aid with a Y-cord, one wire that connects to each ear. It was fine with Joan. The first day that Mary Ellen wore her new aid Joan was excited and expectant. It was just before Christmas, and Mary Ellen was nearly two-and-a-half years old. What a Christmas present it would be! Joan dreamed that she'd turn it on and suddenly Mary Ellen would start talking: "Hello, mama, I'm Mary Ellen Huber." Joan smiled at the thought. It might not be quite like that, but what a difference it would make!

Joan took the kids to market that day. She strapped the aid around Mary Ellen's chest and ran the Y-cord under her dress and out at the throat. Carefully she inserted the ear molds. She watched Mary Ellen's expression, then stood back, waiting. But it was the same Mary Ellen as before, the same beautiful little face, the same blue eyes, and the same light brown curls. There was nothing new. Joan was troubled, fighting back a gnawing sense of disappointment. By the time she and the three kids got to the supermarket, Joan was in a somber mood and so was Mary Ellen. Mary Ellen was suddenly quiet, sitting passively in the shopping cart, not interested in pawing the groceries along the aisles or in the cart. The checkout clerks at the store reacted awkwardly when they saw their favorite hellion wearing a hearing aid. She wasn't bubbly and squirming as she always was.

Joan was becoming increasing alarmed. "What has happened to my little girl?" she asked herself, struggling against tears as they walked up and down the aisles. Later, while the children romped and squabbled at home, Joan sat down at the kitchen table and sobbed. Nothing had changed. Mary Ellen hadn't burst out with words. Joan kept picturing Mary Ellen in the shopping cart with that quizzical look on her face, that expression of pain. "She just sat there staring at me," Joan cried. "She's changed. Her personality isn't the same."

Joan finished her cry and set about making dinner for Dick and the kids. Mary Ellen was still pensive with her new equipment, but Joan was sure it was something she would get used to. She had accustomed herself to so much. It would take Joan many months before she realized that her daughter had turned a corner. It was possibly the biggest breakthrough of Mary Ellen's life. For the first time she was hearing the sounds in the world around her.

7

But what was Mary Ellen hearing? If Joan had listened that day to her daughter's hearing aid, she would have been even more distressed. Sound came through like a badly tuned radio, hissing and crackling. To the normal adult, using a hearing aid is like listening to a scratchy old phonograph record with some sounds difficult or impossible to distinguish. As helpful as this device is, it cannot match the sophistication of the human ear working in conjunction with the brain. The sound of an automobile in the street is as distinct as a human voice a few feet away. The clatter of dishes in the kitchen sounds as though it were in the living room. Was Mary Ellen able to pick up casual conversation? Could she hear distant talk, the way a normal person could? Or was she able to hear only when someone spoke forcefully into her aid? Joan wouldn't know for months.

Sound was a strange dimension to Mary Ellen. Suddenly it burst upon her. She had opened a door and discovered a new realm. The initial impact was confusing, and it would

48

take months, possibly years, to acquaint her with this world. The sound of a door closing, the rustle of leaves on a summer evening, familiar voices; they were nothing more than strange noises to Mary Ellen. She had to learn what they were, to distinguish them from thousands of other sounds that she could now hear.

But where was Joan to begin? In the ensuing months she learned to take Mary Ellen's education a few hours at a time, to look ahead a day at the most.

"Don't expect too much, make a little progress each day, don't overwhelm yourself by hoping for miracles," she kept saying to herself. Instinctively she pumped words into Mary Ellen, repeating them, reinforcing. She was determined that Mary Ellen would learn to speak. Flower, dog, cat, mommy, daddy, brother, sister. . . . It went on and on that first winter and into the spring. She spoke them while Mary Ellen ate her breakfast, repeated them before each morning was out, again in the afternoon, and in the evening before Mary Ellen went to bed. Even when Joan turned to Mike and Kathy, she was aware that Mary Ellen could learn by watching and listening.

Joan developed her own system of flash cards, displaying an object and then repeating its name to the seemingly uncomprehending child. These weren't formal classroom sessions, but whenever Mary Ellen seemed bored or was around her mother, Joan took time to teach a word. It didn't matter where. Mary Ellen learned vocabulary even while sitting on the potty. Joan pasted pictures on the wall around the toilet and she and Mary Ellen talked about them. In the spring Joan included pictures of flowers and described them, but Mary Ellen showed no understanding. But when a few of Joan's crocuses popped up in the front garden, Mary

Ellen noticed. She had seen the flash cards so often, heard the word repeated for weeks. She walked over and bent down to look at them. *"Flauwau,"* she said.

"Hooray, hooray!" Joan yelled. Mary Ellen was progressing. But all too often the struggle seemed hopeless. Mike and Kathy learned more language each day without effort from watching television or playing with their toys. They could pick up a new word or concept in a minute. It would take Mary Ellen a month.

Mary Ellen's handicap was most painful to see around children her own age. On a visit to Dick's cousin, Joan watched sadly as his children chattered with Mike and Kathy while Mary Ellen was unable to make herself understood. Most of the time she pointed to objects she wanted and grunted.

"It's discouraging to bump into a three-year-old who's rattling off language," Joan said to Dick.

Dick was quiet. He spoke little about how Mary Ellen's deafness affected him. But he saw how difficult it was for her to communicate and projected her life twenty years hence. How would she cope? Who would care for her and love her when Joan and Dick were no longer around? Dick restrained his emotions, but occasionally tears welled in his eyes when he thought of his daughter's plight.

Mary Ellen was not nearly so verbal as a normal three-year-old, and even if her pace quickened, her vocabulary would remain limited. It was hard even for family members to accustom themselves to this little deaf child. Joan was aware of their awkwardness around Mary Ellen at the annual Christmas Eve party just after Mary Ellen received her hearing aids.

Joan had an innocent confidence that the instruction

would work. It had to. Besides, Mary Ellen was so eager to learn. She wanted to communicate as desperately as Joan wanted to teach. She ran to her mother when the hearing aid batteries died so that Joan could insert new ones. She was outgoing and wanted to talk, struggling to learn new words. Slowly, week by week, she increased her vocabulary.

But Joan was alone. Doctors weren't able to help, nor were social workers or therapists. Dick and Grandmother offered more encouragement. But they weren't professionals and were just as bewildered as Joan. Joan and her mother constantly dreamed up new teaching techniques over coffee. Only the hearing-aid dealer seemed to offer good advice. He suggested two nearby clinics where Mary Ellen could receive speech therapy, The Helen Beebe Speech and Hearing Clinic in Easton, and the Children's Society which was just around the corner from the Hubers' house, in the same hospital where Mary Ellen had received her first hearing tests. The Children's Society had an opening, and Joan signed up Mary Ellen for one-half hour of therapy each week.

"I'm really pleased with Mary Ellen's setup," Joan told Grandmother Kennedy. "The young man who is her therapist seems very nice."

"What's his background?" Grandmother asked.

"I don't know," Joan replied. "But he has several impressive looking degrees on his wall."

Joan asked few questions and gave no instructions. Who was she to make demands with nothing more than a high school diploma? He was the expert, and Joan trusted him, even though she was ignorant about his method and philosophy of educating the deaf. He took Mary Ellen into a small therapy room and came out half an hour later, always pleased with Mary Ellen's progress.

"She's making excellent headway, Mrs. Huber," he said. "Just keep up the good work."

"Anything in particular I should be doing with her?"

"No, keep working on the hearing. Your persistence seems to be doing nicely."

Mary Ellen had been in therapy four months when spring arrived and with it the news that Joan was pregnant again. She and Dick were pleased, but another child would put additional pressure on Joan and she worried about Mary Ellen. There would be less time for teaching, and the therapist hadn't mentioned future plans for Mary Ellen, or even whether he would be instructing her in the fall. Joan wanted Mary Ellen to continue and hoped the lessons would be expanded to a full hour.

"I'm going to ask the therapist about Mary Ellen's schedule next year," Joan told Grandmother. "With the new baby coming I'd like him to take her for a longer period of time."

"Has the doctor confirmed you're pregnant?" Grandmother asked.

"Oh, yes," Joan replied with a smile. "And everything looks OK this time."

The following day she spoke to the therapist as she and Mary Ellen were leaving his office.

"I'm having another child next winter and I'm hoping you can take Mary Ellen for an hour each week.

He smiled. "Does this make four?"

"Yes," Joan said.

"Congratulations."

"Thank you," Joan replied.

"There's nothing to worry about with Mary Ellen. Have you received the papers yet?"

"No, what papers?" Joan asked.

"For the school."

"What school?"

"The school for the deaf."

"Where's that?"

"In Philadelphia."

"*Philadelphia!* You must be mistaken!" she said. "You've got Mary Ellen mixed up with another child."

"No, no. Mary Ellen is to be enrolled in a residential school for the deaf near Philadelphia. Haven't you been consulted about it yet? It's a wonderful place, like a college campus. The buildings are beautiful. The care for the children is excellent and they have a superb educational program. Mary Ellen will do very well down there."

Thoughts, feelings, fears raced through Joan's head. She visualized Mary Ellen, hardly beyond infancy, lost among the throngs of deaf children at the school. It was cold, impersonal, and she saw Mary Ellen frightened, crying for her family and home. Mary Ellen was not yet three, and this man casually expected her to spend her entire childhood and youth in an institution.

"No!" Joan said. "I won't permit Mary Ellen to go to that school. She won't care how nice a place it is—she'll miss her family."

The therapist was calm, though startled by the vehemence of Joan's refusal. Most parents accepted institutionalization as the best way to deal with their profoundly deaf child. They couldn't help anyway, and left the care to professionals.

"Mrs. Huber, Mary Ellen is profoundly deaf. She can't function in a normal classroom or environment. There's nothing you can do for her. She'll never be able to hear. She'll never acquire speech and language the way a normal person can.

You know how she sounds. She's almost impossible to understand and she can't string two words together."

"But my other two children were incomprehensible when they were learning to speak. Mary Ellen has to learn the same way. She will, too. I know it."

"Mrs. Huber. With all due respect for your courage and tenacity, Mary Ellen will never talk the way a normal person does. People without legs can't walk. The deaf can't be taught to hear. Please be reasonable."

Joan could hardly believe what he was saying. For months he had led her to believe that Mary Ellen would learn to use her hearing and develop language.

"But she's already learned nearly thirty words," Joan interjected.

"Don't be deceived by that. Deaf children tend to learn words in spurts. Mary Ellen is no exception. But she'll never be able to progress much beyond where she is right now. You must accept the fact that your daughter is severely handicapped. She'll never lead a normal life. If you deprive her of other methods of language she'll be without adequate means of communication. She won't be able to speak or sign. She must learn sign language or she'll be lost."

Joan was furious. He had never said Mary Ellen's case was hopeless and she refused to believe that Mary Ellen would never speak. Joan knew enough about schools for the deaf. Mary Ellen couldn't learn language there. She visualized Mary Ellen speaking with her delicate little fingers moving so fast that only someone trained in sign language could understand her. She imagined the hollow, incomprehensible speech. Joan would never be able to converse with her daughter, laugh with her, and confide in her the way Joan did with Grandmother Kennedy, listen to her hopes and aspirations and her sorrows.

Joan grabbed Mary Ellen and turned from the therapist's office. She needed her mother, at home taking care of Mike and Kathy. Normally it was the day Joan, Grandmother, and the children visited Aunt Marge, but not this day. Joan was too upset.

"I know he's wrong, Mom. I know it, but no one will agree with me," Joan cried. "She'll speak someday. We'll do it. Why does everyone insist that we can't?"

Joan sat down, exhausted. There had to be alternatives. She'd find them. Grandmother agreed as Joan talked out loud, exploring the possibilities.

"If only I knew someone who could help. Isn't there any-one in this world who knows anything about deafness?"

"Do you know any families with deaf children?" Grand-mother asked.

Joan thought a moment.

"No. *No, wait!* There is someone." Joan's eyes became bright. "That little girl at church. You know, the one with the hearing aids. She's deaf. I know she goes to Notre Dame School because she wears a school uniform."

Occasionally Joan saw her, coming into church with the long strands of wire hanging down from her ears and disap-pearing into her dress, where they attached to the aid. She and Grandmother both had noticed. Even with aids she acted like a normal girl. Most important, she was at home. Joan would find her.

"Joan, please don't overdo it," Grandmother cautioned. "You've got that new baby to think about. Remember what the doctor said. It won't be an easy pregnancy."

But there was no way to slow Joan down. She became a sleuth. She called the school and they gave her the child's name—Marianne Derr—and was told she lived nearby. Joan got the address and the next morning Joan walked boldly up to the Derrs' front door and rang the bell. Kathryn Derr answered. She was a small woman with a warm face. She was startled by the presence of a woman on the front porch.

Joan's tone betrayed her desperation. "Mrs. Derr, I'm Joan Huber. I have a deaf child and I've seen your daughter in church. I've just been told that my daughter should be institutionalized. I need your help. I can't let my daughter be taken away."

Kathyrn Derr smiled. She extended her arm to welcome Joan inside. "Come in, come in, my dear, I've heard that story so often."

Joan still expected Kathryn to say there was nothing to be done. Instead, she was encouraging.

"Joan, I've been through the same thing. Marianne was born profoundly deaf and my husband and I almost gave up hope. Then we found the Beebe clinic in Easton."

"I heard about that clinic from our hearing-aid dealer," Joan said. She was unable to hold back the tears. She described the years of search and finally the conversation with the therapist.

Kathryn, too, had searched for alternatives to institutionalization. For several years she had looked, and finally she and her husband decided the only answer was to move to St. Louis to be near the St. Joseph's Institute for the Deaf, one of the few schools in the country that stressed the development of hearing and speech. Then she had met a mother whose son was enrolled in the Beebe clinic.

"Helen Beebe has a long history in deaf education. What distinguishes her from most others is that she believes that deaf children, even the most profoundly deaf, can be taught to hear and speak. Marianne has been in Beebe's clinic for several years, and her progress is remarkable. But Beebe's older students are even better. Some are able to hear with relative ease and their speech is nearly perfect. Beebe is taking a new batch of children handicapped by the epidemic of rubella that affected your Mary Ellen."

While Joan sat in the Derrs' living room, Kathryn picked up the phone and called the Beebe clinic. Within minutes Joan had an appointment to meet Helen Beebe the next day.

8

JOAN DROVE FROM ALLENTOWN, down the four-lane divided
highway, around Bethlehem to Easton, fifteen miles to the
east at the confluence of the Delaware and Lehigh rivers. Its
history now obscured, Easton was once a major center in a
young United States. During the Revolutionary War it was a
supply depot and hosted many of the Founding Fathers, including Washington and Franklin, who passed through to
skirt British-held territory across the Delaware in New
Jersey. In the nineteenth century it became a center of com-
merce, the terminus of the Lehigh, Delaware, and Morris ca-
nals, and the site of one of the largest iron foundries in the
nation. Little remained of its past grandeur except the many
stately and large houses in the downtown and on College
Hill, which rose above the city of 27,000 people.

The Beebe clinic was situated on the hill in a small, one-
story building two blocks from Lafayette College. Joan and
Mary Ellen entered a small waiting room. There was little
else beyond, a bathroom and two therapy rooms, one of
which doubled as Helen Beebe's office. Joan heard voices,

children and therapists at work. She waited a few minutes before Beebe appeared, a woman different from Joan's expectations. She was tall, nearly six feet, and reedlike. She carried herself erect and maintained an aura of authority, though it was not overbearing. Her intelligent gray eyes and graying hair lent her an air of wisdom beyond her years. Her voice was youthful for a woman in her mid-fifties.

"Mrs. Huber? I'm Helen Beebe. Hello, Mary Ellen," Beebe said.

"Hello," Mary Ellen answered.

Beebe looked at Joan, her face registering approval. "She does well," Beebe said.

"We've worked hard on her vocabulary," Joan said.

"And you've worked on her hearing too, I see," Beebe replied. Mary Ellen smiled as she and Joan followed Beebe into her office. The room was simply decorated, with several pictures on the walls and a bookcase with works on hearing and speech and photographs on the shelves. Joan told Beebe about Mary Ellen, the therapist, Kathryn Derr, and her determination that Mary Ellen would not be sent away to a school for the deaf.

Joan's story was familiar to Beebe. How many mothers with deaf children had wound up on her doorstep with similar tales, desperate because they had no place to turn? The mothers believed there was something better for their children than schools for the deaf and sign language. Beebe had seen cases where physicians had placed deaf children in homes for the retarded because they had misdiagnosed the handicap.

Beebe said there was hope; she manufactured it with her own efforts. She told Joan how she had taken profoundly deaf children, developed their residual hearing, and taught them language. There was nothing magical about it. It was logical, she said, and if deaf educators were open-minded, they would realize that deaf children could be taught to hear and speak.

"Mary Ellen shows good potential," Beebe said. "And there's every reason to believe she will continue to improve. Does she ever wear two aids?" Beebe asked.

"She's just been using the one," Joan replied.

"Eventually she should have two. Binaural amplification is much better," Beebe said.

"The audiologist at the hospital in Philadelphia said there was no point in aiding the right ear," Joan said. "They said it was dead."

"One thing you must remember from the start, Joan, and you already know this or you wouldn't be here. Don't listen to everything the doctors and audiologists tell you. Many don't believe deaf children can be taught to use their hearing and to speak. Even when I show them my students, they refuse to believe it. They say they're only moderately deaf. When I show them the audiograms, they say the child is exceptional. But I take all my children as they come in off the street. There's no selection process here. We don't weed out children who might not make it. Not all do, but most succeed. About eighty percent of our students are successfully mainstreamed with good speaking and hearing skills. Mary Ellen will be able to go to school and be like most normal children. She'll hear and speak just like any other child. You can expect Mary Ellen to be normal."

The news put Joan in an ebullient mood. Beebe was so confident. "I'm getting it straight. There's no baloney in this," Joan told herself.

"But," Beebe cautioned, "it will take a tremendous effort on your part. Teaching Mary Ellen will require a total commitment. You must use every waking minute to train her.

And that's the responsibility of the parents, not the clinic. I punch out every night at five. You will seldom have a rest from your work. But if you succeed, you will have a child who speaks and hears instead of one who uses sign language."

Joan had instinctively followed the right prescription, but it had to be more intense, more concentrated. One major ingredient was discipline. No deaf child ever succeeded without discipline. Deaf children, Beebe stressed, were masters at using their handicap to get attention and sympathy. There could be none of that with Mary Ellen, or any deaf child. Their work was cut out and the effort would go on for years.

Joan wanted to enroll Mary Ellen then, but it was already June and the clinic was winding down before it closed in August for a month. Mary Ellen was accepted in September for a course of therapy that included two hour-long sessions each week. The therapy would continue, on varying schedules, well into her teenage years.

Joan was jubilant when she left the clinic. She had searched for this woman for three years and Beebe literally had been under her nose. Why hadn't anyone recommended her before?

"I've found this marvelous speech specialist in Easton who works with deaf kids," Joan told the therapist at the Children's Society.

"You mean Mrs. Beebe."

"You know about her?" Joan was surprised.

"Oh, yes. She's a competitor."

"Why didn't you tell me about her? She's terrific."

"It doesn't work, Joan. Don't be fooled by her claims. Deaf children can't be taught to hear. It's impossible. Besides, she's expensive, and the therapy will disrupt your family and you won't have enough time to devote to your other children."

"That's my decision, not yours," Joan said angrily. "I'll spend my time as I please and if it's too expensive we'll rob banks. How can you call her your competition? You have a child the same age. How would you feel if your family doctor refused to recommend a specialist because he was competition? You can't play with people's lives like that."

"Mrs. Huber, I don't agree with her method. It doesn't work. If it were possible many more would be doing so. Quite frankly, Mrs. Beebe is the first person who has told you what you want to hear. The rest of us are telling you the truth."

The same doubts lingered; so did the fear. Joan rushed home to Dick.

"How could he say that? How can he do that? Professionals don't understand. If there's any chance that Mary Ellen can learn to hear and speak, they should be the ones to recommend this possibility first, not last."

Maybe the therapist was right. Joan and Dick had no way of knowing. They couldn't say whether deaf children could be taught to hear and speak like other normal children, but they had to give it a try. They would send Mary Ellen to the Beebe clinic for a year. If there was no demonstrable progress by that time, they could take her out and place her in more traditional therapy. That had to be the last resort. Mary Ellen was eager to learn and was able to hear. How else could she speak any words at all?

"The responsibility for all this will fall on you. I can't give up my work. Can you handle it?" Dick had asked.

"I want to give the clinic a try," Joan said. She thought for a moment. "My gut tells me it can be done. It's just that so many doubts have been planted. So many people who deal with deafness say it will never work. What we're doing is like defying God. They are the experts and yet I know they are wrong. And Beebe is the first person who ever acknowledged that I was right."

The therapy was expensive, about $1,000 a year, but Dick and Joan would manage. Joan was also concerned because she hadn't heard from Beebe and just prayed she would not forget about Mary Ellen.

The strain took its toll. In June, Joan's doctor ordered her to bed to try and save her baby. But in vain. Joan miscarried and would never realize her dream of four children. Mary Ellen was to be their last.

It was early September, just after Mary Ellen's third birthday, when she and Joan began the twice weekly treks to the Beebe clinic. Joan soon found out that Beebe expected double the effort she and Mary Ellen were accustomed to, but Mary Ellen didn't seem to mind.

"She takes to Mrs. Beebe like a duck takes to water," Joan told Grandmother. "She's so eager to communicate I'm certain she will do well there."

Everything Mary Ellen learned gave Joan such satisfaction. It was a relief to see her daughter in an environment where she was encouraged to use her hearing. Joan couldn't believe there were so many people who said it was impossible, who claimed that Beebe was an impostor and that her successful students really were children with minimal hearing loss. Joan had met several of Beebe's other students, some Mary Ellen's age, who had been in therapy for months. David Davis, who had been Beebe's patient for two and a half years, was just as deaf as Mary Ellen, but he could hear well and his language was good.

"How could all those people out there be so wrong?" Joan asked herself. "How could they be so certain of themselves?"

Beebe was impressed with Mary Ellen's progress, since most of her children arrived virtually unable to speak. Mary Ellen was doing well at the clinic, learning words and adding to her vocabulary during the summer. The clinic expected every child to improve his vocabulary when the clinic closed for August. But Beebe was never satisfied with a child's development until it was almost perfect. The therapy was rigorous and demanding to the point where even enthusiasts like Mary Ellen soon cooled. Beebe had seen the therapy work and knew it was the children's only salvation.

Joan began formal lessons with Mary Ellen several times a day and learned to plan the sessions in advance. This meant laying out toys, pictures, puzzles, and books that were useful in teaching language. She also learned to move quickly from subject to subject to hold Mary Ellen's attention. If Joan was lucky, Mary Ellen would respond to an object.

"Bus," Joan said. "Bus, bus."

"Ba . . . Ba," came the reply.

"Bus, bus!"

"Ba . . . ba."

"Look at the car, Mary Ellen. This is a toy *car!*"

There was no reply.

"Car," Joan repeated.

Still no response.

Joan moved on.

"Mary Ellen must start using sentences," Beebe told Joan. "She's not going to get anywhere unless she can put those words to use."

It was the kind of challenge that Beebe threw at her parents matter-of-factly and expected them to perform without protest. Teaching Mary Ellen words was hard enough. But sentences, abstractions, verbs, that was different. How did you do that? Joan would learn. She would just have to do the best she could.

She began one day at lunchtime. Grandmother was expected, and Mary Ellen went over to the cupboard and pointed to one of her favorite soups.

"Doup, doup," she said, her slender finger pointing to one of the shelves.

"Mary Ellen, from now on you are going to speak in sentences when you want something. You must say, 'I want soup.'"

"Doup, doup," came Mary Ellen's reply.

"I want soup," Joan said slowly.

"Doup, doup."

Mary Ellen began to shriek and thrash about. Grandmother walked in on the raging contest. Joan knew she couldn't give in. She was learning the method well. Discipline and hard work, that was the only way deaf children would succeed. It was Beebe's prescription.

9

BEEBE, AS SHE WAS known by all, taking her name from her former husband, was born Helen Hulick and raised in and around Easton. She attended Easton High School and later the Miss Choate School in Brookline, Massachusetts, near Boston. She was the product of an era when proper young ladies went on to finishing school. She continued to Wellesley, but became bored and dropped out at the end of her sophomore year to enroll in the teacher training program at the Clark School for the Deaf in Northampton, Massachusetts. It looked more interesting than Wellesley, but the near monastic life-style among deaf children and the Victorian ladies who ran the school soon became tiresome. Beebe was proper, but not that proper, and she yearned to kick up her heels. Occasionally she would slip across the state line to Keene, New Hampshire, to visit friends.

In the 1920s the Clark School was a cluster of four structures, a classroom building and three dormitories situated on Round Hill in the town of Northampton. It was a "traditional oral" school for the deaf, where students were taught speech rather than sign language. The children arrived at six or seven years of age with little or no training. A decade later they graduated, most with low proficiency in speech and virtually no hearing. There was little hope that they would ever lead normal lives. Just trying to understand them was an effort, and Beebe always thought they sounded like people talking with strong foreign accents.

The problem wasn't solely the school's fault. These were the days before hearing aids, and some educators of the deaf believed that with amplified sound deaf children could hear. They speculated that if exposed long enough, these children might be able to acquire speech and language. But the ear horns used at Clark and elsewhere were a far cry from today's modern hearing aids. Several times a week Beebe conducted hearing training, speaking to individual students through one of the horns. But she was affected by the hopelessness of the situation, the fact that most of the children would remain severely handicapped throughout their lives.

In 1932 Beebe left Clark and headed west, via the Panama Canal to San Francisco. She would have stayed in the Bay area, but the jobs were elsewhere. She went to Oregon to a school for the deaf in Salem. It was little different from Clark. Beebe experienced the same frustrating struggle to teach the children and the same conservative attitude among the staff. She moved on, working her way closer to San Francisco, this time to the Sacramento School for the Deaf. It was an unusual school, remarkably different from Clark and Salem. Sacramento was a day school and the students returned home each night, to their parents and brothers and sisters. Beebe was impressed by how natural they were, how much more aware and advanced than their counterparts at Clark and Salem. Her observations greatly influenced her approach to deaf education.

Her experience in Sacramento laid the foundation for her belief that all deaf children should be mainstreamed from the outset, and that without exposure to the world they would never learn to speak naturally. She learned that among the deaf, the deaf can learn to speak only like the deaf.

In 1934 Beebe finally arrived back in San Francisco, where she taught at the Berkeley School for the Deaf. By this time, however, her interest had waned and she left teaching altogether in 1936 when she married Kenneth Beebe. The couple moved to Sonoma and the Valley of the Moon, where Kenneth pursued a life-long dream to be a cattle rancher and where Beebe was the chef for ranch hands and family. But the dream faded, and the Beebes moved back to San Francisco, where Kenneth went into the insurance business. Beebe began tutoring deaf children and took courses at Stanford, studying aspects of personality as revealed through voice and speech. Her professor was Dr. Paul Moses and their meeting was a fateful one for Beebe.

Helen and Kenneth Beebe were divorced in 1942, and Beebe returned to Easton to live with her mother in the second-floor apartment of a large Georgian-style house on College Hill. She carried a letter of introduction from Dr. Moses to Dr. Emil Froeschels, a Vienna-born speech and voice pathologist who practiced in New York.

Before the war broke out in Europe in 1939, Dr. Froeschels had developed a worldwide reputation as a leader in speech and voice pathology, not unlike Freud's reputation as a psychoanalyst, and the two had been acquainted in Vienna. Froeschels had directed his own speech and voice clinic with more than twenty-five assistants, and patients came from around the world for treatment and therapy. But the Nazi takeover of Austria forced him to flee, first to the Netherlands and then to the United States, where he took a position at the Central Institute for the Deaf in St. Louis. But he found himself at odds with the philosophy of the institution and moved to New York to start a private practice in 1940.

When Beebe and Froeschels met in 1942, they were both adrift. Beebe needed a strong mentor, and Froeschels, who had been used to dominating a staff of young physicians, needed a student. He missed the deferential treatment traditionally given an important physician in Europe. In the United States he had lost his following and his importance. Froeschels was thickly built, in his middle fifties, and something of a Renaissance man. He had trained as a physician, specializing in pediatrics and neurology, but he had also ventured into philosophy, publishing several works. As a young doctor, Froeschels had chosen to concentrate on the study of voice and speech because few physicians entered the field and no one was trained to deal with the multitude of speech and voice problems.

With her introduction in hand, Beebe ventured into New York one spring day in 1942 to meet this Viennese physician, who greeted her with characteristic Germanic bluntness.

"What can I do for you? I suppose you don't know yourself." Beebe didn't know, but the meeting was successful, and she began a professional relationship with Froeschels that was to last thirty years. He would become like a father, and, as in the era when physicians gained their knowledge through a long apprenticeship, Beebe became Froeschels' private pupil. In his office in the Wickersham Building on Fifty-eighth Street in Manhattan, he would lecture her on the anatomy of voice and the general nature of speech. Twice weekly she accompanied him to the speech and voice clinic at Mount Sinai Hospital, observing his treatment of a wide range of patients and problems—stutterers, clutterers, patients with delayed speech and aphasia. As part of her training, Froeschels suggested Beebe take up singing so that she could eventually treat singers with voice problems. He arranged for the lessons with an elderly Viennese teacher who had escaped from Vienna just ahead of the Nazis and come to New York to join the growing Austrian community there. Beebe found she could sing and learned a repertoire of German songs by such masters as Brahms, Schubert, and Schumann.

By 1944 Beebe had started her own part-time practice, spending two days a week in a small clinic at Easton Hospital and three days as Froeschels' assistant in New York, working with his patients, completing office work, and editing his papers. It was strenuous, commuting to and from Easton by train, and the shortages created by the war made it more difficult. She remained in New York Tuesday, Wednesday, and Thursday, and then returned to work on cases at home. One of her first was a brain-damaged child in Easton whose parents had given up hope of ever controlling his behavior. They were told by doctors not to use discipline and relegated him to the upstairs, where he lived like a wild beast, his room in a shambles. But this meant virtually shackling him whenever he was fed or taken outdoors. Beebe was ideal for the assignment, having always believed discipline was the secret to learning. Over a period of time she was able to instill a measure of civility in the boy.

Beebe had few patients with speech and voice problems when she first opened her clinic, but slowly the caseload grew, mostly from physician referrals. Many patients were stroke victims, men and women who had to regain their ability to speak. Others suffered from a variety of speech problems, stuttering being one of the most common. Deafness, however, was not an affliction that Beebe expected to take much of her time. There was so little hope for any deaf child, and the opportunities were limited to state schools. But serendipity played a major role in changing Beebe's life.

Not long after her return from San Francisco, Beebe was asked to examine the daughter of a neighbor who lived across the street. Mardie Crannell seemed like a healthy child when she was born, but it soon became apparent that she was not developing communication skills. She didn't talk at all and had many of the characteristics of a deaf child. Beebe suggested that Mardie be examined by Dr. Froeschels, who espoused a novel theory that any deaf child could be taught to hear through residual hearing. It was considered revolutionary at the time, though it had been known for more than a century.

Froeschels had learned the concept from Victor Urbantschitsch, a Viennese physician at the turn of the century who postulated that all deaf children have a small remnant of auditory ability, no matter how deaf they are. It was believed that this auditory remnant could be developed and expanded so that the deaf child could be taught to hear. But before the 1940s and the advent of the wearable hearing aid, there was no way the theory could be tested. So it remained unproved and controversial. Most educators of the deaf, seeing the years of effort that went into teaching even the rudiments of language, scoffed at the idea that the deaf could be taught to hear. Factions developed between the oralists, who believed the deaf could be taught to hear and speak, and those who relied on the manual methods of teaching communication, such as sign language and lipreading.

Froeschels tested Mardie with a series of wooden whistles, standing behind her and blowing each one, which had a different pitch. He picked up one after another and blew them with varying force and at various distances from her ears. Mardie was unable to hear the tones, and it was obvious that she was profoundly deaf.

Beebe agreed to embark on an experiment that twenty years later would occupy all her time. But in 1944 she had no experience in applying the theory of residual hearing and no prescription for Mardie. She didn't even have a name for her teaching method. She started from scratch, working it out as she went along. Most disturbing of all, however, was the fact that all her years in deaf education and all the experience were of little use. In 1944, when Beebe began to teach Mardie, there was virtually no one in the country educating deaf children using the theory of residual hearing. The few other pioneers in the field were, like Beebe, young professionals in the early stages of their practice.

It was Mardie's mother who had most of the responsibility. In later years, parent participation became the basic tenet of Beebe's method; otherwise there was little chance the child would succeed. In 1944 hearing aids were powered by dry-cell batteries that were large even for adults. One young man carried the battery in a pants pocket, but soon refused to use his aid because his pants kept falling down. Until Mardie received her own aid, Mrs. Crannell and Beebe introduced her to sound using a homemade hearing aid fashioned from a length of rubber hose, fitted at one end with an ear olive, a small earpiece, and at the other with a standard kitchen funnel. The aid intensified sound in the same manner as a stethoscope. The olive was inserted into the ear, and Mrs. Crannell and Beebe began feeding sound to Mardie. Syllables came first: *ma ma ma ma ma; da da da da da; fa fa fa fa fa; ba ba ba ba ba*—over and over and over. It would take years, and as Joan found out with Mary

72

Ellen, deaf children don't suddenly start using language the minute they are introduced to sound. They must become familiar with it and learn what it is, what each sound means and the appropriate response required.

Mrs. Crannell began the instruction with a ball, a toy car, and two small dolls, one representing a boy, the other a girl. Three times a day for half an hour, she sat opposite Mardie, picking up each object, naming it and handing it to her daughter. She would then retrieve it and pick up the next object and name that. At first Mrs. Crannell spoke into the hearing tube, but later Mardie was fitted with a hearing aid. It was a bulky contraption; Mrs. Crannell made Mardie a special jacket with two large pockets, one for a microphone, the other for the two heavy dry cell batteries. The microphone was placed on Mardie's chest and the batteries went on her back. Because of the size of the hearing aid, only one ear could be assisted, making it more difficult for Mardie to acquire speech and language with the facility of Beebe's later students, who had smaller, more powerful binaural aids, one for each ear.

Mardie had not heard sound for the first eighteen months of her life, and Beebe and Mrs. Crannell had no idea whether their efforts would produce anything. The weeks went by. Every day Mardie was reintroduced to the ball and the dolls. Every day was the same, no response. But the eighth week brought a breakthrough. Finally Mardie understood and picked up the correct object, demonstrating that she was hearing well enough to distinguish between objects. But just learning the basics would take months. Mrs. Crannel began by introducing simple commands: "Pick it up," "Put it back," and "Come here." Mardie was expected to respond to questions such as "Where is Daddy?" and "Where is the light?"

In the first year Beebe was the consultant rather than the teacher, providing Mrs. Crannell with direction and reinforcement whenever she needed it. Mardie began formal training sessions with Beebe a year later when she was three. The therapy seemed to be working; the words were coming more rapidly, not always intelligible, but Mardie understood them and was able to use a few such as "bye-bye," "hi," and "Mommie." Her hearing also was developing, and within a year she was able to hear her name called from a distance. But the test was whether Mardie could ever be taught to speak like a normal adult. Would she ever develop the melody and rhythm of normal speech? Beebe didn't stress articulation in Mardie's training. Her chief concern was that Mardie learn to speak spontaneously with as much normal inflection and melody in her speech as possible. They could leave the articulation till later.

This was a far different approach than anything Beebe had learned at the schools for the deaf. At Clark, Salem, and the others, the children had learned to articulate every word and pronounce each with great precision. Articulation of the word automobile, for instance, would have been taught placing emphasis on each syllable—*aw–toe–moe–beal.* But Beebe knew that when a deaf child learned to speak in this fashion, few people were able to understand. It was artificial language. Instead of saying a sentence, as the normal person would, the deaf child strung out every word, stressing each syllable.

Beebe realized that if the deaf child were allowed to imitate natural sounds and phrases, he or she would pick up the proper melody and be comprehensible, even though some of the syllables might be incorrectly pronounced. The word automobile might come out *audomobeal,* but would be spoken with sufficient melody and fluency to be understood.

This was true of Mardie. She began speaking with a normal inflection even though her articulation was not perfect, and after several years Mrs. Crannell understood most of what Mardie was saying. "The children she plays with used to say, 'Mardie doesn't talk.' Now they say, 'Mardie doesn't speak well!'" Mrs. Crannell told Beebe.

Mardie was the first of scores of deaf children who would undergo hour-long therapy sessions with Beebe, twice a week for as long as fifteen years. Grueling though they were, the therapy sessions were the only road to success.

Day in, day out, Mardie's therapy continued, at home or in Beebe's two-room clinic, which was now located on Cattell Street, not far from the Crannells' College Hill home. Beebe was developing her therapy for deaf children, and it was slow and laborious work. She patiently repeated words, sounds, syllables. She placed objects on the table and expected Mardie to pick them up after they were named. She put toy farm animals in front of Mardie and asked her to select one after she imitated its sounds.

"What goes moo, moo, moo?" Beebe asked. The small therapy room was filled with moos, baas, clucks and quacks. Wrapped in her cumbersome jacket that held her aid, Mardie listened intently and tried to pick out the right animal.

Progress was slow, but steady and encouraging. Whenever Beebe needed direction or new ideas, she turned to Froeschels for advice and he offered suggestions. Beebe and Froeschels agreed that Mardie should be mainstreamed as quickly as possible, to get her in school and social situations with children her age. She was four years old when enrolled in the College Hill Presbyterian Church nursery school a few blocks from home. She mingled easily with her classmates, and Mrs. Crannell was gratified to see her daughter doing so well. She could print, read some words, count, and name the different colors. She understood most ordinary conversations and was able to follow children's stories being read in class. Mardie also did not speak with a heavy deaf accent. The months and years of effort had produced a more natural pitch and more normal speech melody instead of the strained, generally incomprehensible language of the deaf.

Mardie was not allowed to lip-read, a natural instinct of all deaf children, and the prohibition against it would remain a major principle of Beebe's method, astounding many educators of the deaf. After all, they charged, it was like prohibiting a blind child from using touch to learn of the world around him. Beebe reasoned, however, that if Mardie were allowed to lip-read, it would jeopardize the development of her hearing. The rationale of the therapy was that Mardie was forced to listen to everything that she heard. Listen, listen, listen—that was becoming the catchword of Beebe's method. She said it dozens of times during a therapy session, softly, then sternly when Mardie's concentration drifted. Beebe noticed that when she spoke, Mardie focused on her lips, trying to pick out the words she couldn't hear. Beebe quickly developed a countermeasure by holding her hand up to cover her mouth.

Mardie's development and progress were to have an ironic effect on Beebe. The former teacher of the deaf who hoped to establish a reputation and practice in speech and voice therapy was finding success back in deaf education. Mardie was not the only child who came to Beebe. Within a short period, other families brought their deaf children to the clinic, seeking some way to overcome the handicap.

10

"WHERE'S THE DOG, Mary Ellen? Where's the dog? The dog goes woof, woof, woof." Beebe and Mary Ellen sat at a small table in the enclosed therapy room, Beebe's tall frame stuck awkwardly in a small chair, her knees jutting above the child's table.

"Let's pay attention, Mary Ellen," Beebe admonished gently. "The dog goes woof, woof, woof. Hand me the dog, Mary Ellen." She pointed to a group of miniature farm animals on the table, a dog, a horse, a cow, and a pig.

"You must force her to listen," Beebe reminded Joan constantly at their conferences. "You may find that you have to guide her hand to the right object, but eventually she'll understand and pick it up."

Mary Ellen yawned. "Pay attention, Mary Ellen." Beebe reached over and took Mary Ellen's hand and gently guided it to the toy dog. Mary Ellen picked it up and Beebe instructed her to place it in the box where the animals were kept.

"Listen, Mary Ellen. *L–i–s–t–e–n*. Moo, moo, moo. What goes moo, moo, moo?"

Mary Ellen did not respond. Beebe picked up a small box of raisins and placed several on the table near the animals. Mary Ellen reached for one, but Beebe quickly grabbed her hand.

"Not until you tell me what goes moo. Moo, moo, moo," Beebe said.

Mary Ellen remained mute, and Beebe repeated the animal sound: "Moo, moo, moo. Mary Ellen, what goes moo?" Mary Ellen continued to stare blankly at Beebe. Beebe reached over and took a raisin and plopped it in her mouth. Mary Ellen began to cry.

"You've got to keep her attention," Beebe told Joan afterward. "Keep her occupied and pour in the language. Don't be afraid to make these silly animal sounds. If you stimulate the remnant of hearing she has, it will develop and she will become a hearing, speaking child."

Beebe and Joan met frequently to review Mary Ellen's progress, Beebe always demanding more and offering strategies to improve Mary Ellen's learning. The prescription was always the same, more hard work. Joan listened without protest, but there were times when she felt she could go no further. She spent the entire day working with Mary Ellen, pumping her full of language, words, syllables, animal grunts, and noises. What more could she do?

"Make those animal sounds with ooh's and aah's," Beebe said. "Throw them out with different pitches. You must force her to listen, over and over and over," Beebe said. "You hope that she'll retain the word or sound you've concentrated on and hand you the cow or the dog or the pig. When she's learned animal sounds move on to name them."

It seemed an incredible task. "Your purpose is to stimulate the receptive centers of the brain," Beebe said. "Just pump in sounds, words, phrases. You know Mary Ellen is not getting it all, but someday she'll learn that if she vocalizes she can make something happen."

It was slow, but Joan was beginning to see it work. "Mary Ellen has been asking for cookies instead of screaming for them. She's starting to realize that asking for them gets faster action," Joan wrote in her diary in the first weeks after Mary Ellen had started at the Beebe clinic.

September 9. Made my first attempt at reading a story to Mary Ellen. She selected a pussycat book. Can't say that I'm real happy with the first sitting. She, of course, was in charge, turning the pages. We will try again but not immediately. Progress . . . Mary Ellen made a good attempt at a sentence, "go bye-bye—car?"

September 10. Had a grand day . . . no competition . . . Kathy and Mike were away for the day. Mary Ellen and I visited Grandmother and Aunt Marge. While at Aunt Marge's, Mary Ellen's cousins came and taught her their games from kindergarten. We all played London Bridge, Ring Around the Rosie, and Little Sally Water. Mary Ellen caught on and enjoyed.

But learning games wasn't always easy for Mary Ellen. She tried to play hide-and-seek with Mike and Kathy, but didn't understand the rules and they refused to let her join in. Joan was ready when Mary Ellen came in crying. She knew that informal instruction was the best way to teach, and she and Mary Ellen played hide-and-seek around the house. Joan hid behind the bed while changing the sheets, in the shower when picking up the laundry, in closets, behind doors and furniture. Then she made Mary Ellen hide. Mary Ellen was delighted by the new game.

Joan became Mary Ellen's steadfast playmate as well as teacher. The mornings were the best time to instruct when the children came down and congregated in the playroom while Joan worked in the kitchen. It was only a matter of time before Mary Ellen came in asking questions or complaining because of a scuffle with her sister or brother.

"What do you have there?" Joan asked. "Mary Ellen, that's a feather, *f–e–a–t–h–e–r*. *F–e–a–t–h–e–r–s* come from birds. Can you say *f–e–a–t–h–e–r*, Mary Ellen? *F–e–a–t–h–e–r*."

"*Fevver,*" Mary Ellen replied.

"Hooray! That's terrific," Joan cried.

Grandmother Kennedy also worked with Mary Ellen when she came for coffee or when she sat for the kids. She was becoming as good a teacher as Joan.

"Progress!!" Joan wrote in her diary. "Mary Ellen sat on my lap with Mike's weekly paper from school. It was great material loaded with good, clear, colorful pictures. When asked, Mary Ellen pointed out the following: bear, lion, dog, pussycat, chicken, pig, children praying, and leaves. She made counting noises trying to count the leaves and the children. She did all this because Mike and Kathy did it first. Competition. I'm finding out this is Mary Ellen's biggest helper. I think if possible it would be great if all mothers like myself could get themselves a little helpmate. This seems to break down the barriers of learning faster, with less effort."

But when Joan critically analyzed Mary Ellen's progress, she sometimes despaired. Yes, Mary Ellen pointed to the pictures and turned the pages. But she couldn't say the names of the animals in the book. She gave them mumbo-jumbo names. It was the same with numbers and letters.

Mary Ellen continued to be Joan's "helpmate." If they were doing the laundry, Mary Ellen learned the names of various articles of clothing.

"This is a shirt, Mary Ellen. Shirt. And these are pants, p–a–n–t–s. Pants, Mary Ellen." If they did the dishes it was the same. "Glass, Mary Ellen. This is a glass."

It was a one-way conversation, and if Mary Ellen responded, frequently it was gibberish. For hours she would babble on in her own fabricated language, demanding that everyone listen. Joan called it little Indian talk, and it was amusing at times. Mary Ellen sat at the dinner table jabbering away in her alien language while the other family members conversed in English. The little Indian talk got louder and louder until all other conversation was drowned out and Joan put a stop to it. The little Indian jabbered all the way to Beebe's, but she stopped when Mary Ellen entered the clinic where Beebe clamped down and required her to speak her native tongue.

The gibberish accentuated the struggle. She knew words and Joan was proud of her vocabulary, but it was so limited.

"Sometimes I'm just terrified that Mary Ellen will reach a plateau and never go beyond it," Joan said to Dick one evening after the children were in bed. They sat together on the small patio just outside the kitchen and relaxed in the warm evening of early fall. The sky to the west over Allentown was a deepening red. An airplane circled low nearby, on its approach to the Allentown-Bethlehem-Easton Airport several miles to the north.

"Her little Indian talk is beginning to worry me. Will she

ever grow out of it? I keep thinking that maybe she'll get stuck in some phase," Joan said.

"Do any of Beebe's other kids get stuck and never get out of it?" Dick asked.

"Don't think so," Joan replied.

"Well, then let's not worry about it. It probably won't happen."

They were silent for a few moments. Dick knew Joan was thinking about Mary Ellen. She couldn't escape it. At least he had his work. Joan lived Mary Ellen twenty-four hours a day.

"How am I ever going to teach her?" Joan asked in despair. *"How, how, how?"*

Sure, some of the kids failed. Some were just so deaf they would never acquire language even with aids. Others failed because of some unknown predilection. Others rebelled. But deep down Joan believed the biggest cause of failure was parents who gave up or wore out. That was Joan's fear and it haunted her. She remembered Beebe's words and those of another clinic therapist.

"Some parents come into the program and say they can't do it," one therapist reported. "Others simply fail at the job. One mother didn't like children. She never intended to have a child and then was stuck with one who was deaf. She didn't enjoy working with him. She hated it. It was work and she despised it and there was no joy in it for her. The therapy ground to a halt, and that's not her fault or his fault. That's God's fault."

"You do it," Beebe replied the next day. "I can help you. But you've got to do it." Joan would take Mary Ellen home and shut out the fears and knuckle down to work again. She lived by her motto not to look too far into the future. While most children Mary Ellen's age were learning whole sentences, Mary Ellen lagged badly.

"One day at a time," Joan kept reminding herself. "One day at a time."

No matter how tired she was, no matter how ineffective the day's teaching seemed to be, she pushed on, sometimes amused, sometimes laughing with Mary Ellen, frequently scolding her for her behavior, sometimes on the brink of despair. But she knew she had to keep going. It was Mary Ellen's only chance.

"Progress . . . a sentence, "'Grandma—sit down,'" Joan wrote in her diary September 12, 1967. Mary Ellen was three years old.

September 13. Grandma says Mary Ellen said 'Dixie cup.'

September 14. Bad day with tantrums. I'll excuse them because Mary Ellen is just getting over a sore throat.

She shouldn't excuse Mary Ellen. The child had to learn, but it was difficult for Joan to be so tough. So much was demanded of Mary Ellen, more than Joan had ever expected of Mike and Kathy. She asked Mary Ellen to repeat constantly to assure herself that she had learned a word or a phrase. Few parents asked this of their hearing children. They assumed the child learned on first hearing. But the parent of a deaf child needs the reinforcement as much as the child.

11

TWICE A WEEK Mary Ellen underwent an hour of rigorous therapy. Not once during that hour could she relax. Beebe demanded, coaxed, drilled, and scolded. No student anywhere had such a demanding regimen.

Joan listened carefully those first months that Mary Ellen was enrolled in the clinic and watched Beebe or Antoinette ("Guffie") Goffredo, Beebe's assistant, through the small glass window in the therapy room. She sought Beebe's advice and direction whenever Beebe had a spare moment. Slowly she began to understand the strategy behind the therapy. There was reason for all the woofing, quacking, and mooing, the syllables, the words, the sentences, the discipline, the tears, and the cheering whenever Mary Ellen did well. At the outset the team of therapists alerted Mary Ellen to sound, so simple a concept for a hearing person to understand, but almost impossible to describe to a deaf child. Mary Ellen could barely hear the world around her with her aids.

Animal noises weren't the only techniques used to alert

Mary Ellen to sound. Beebe would hold marbles up for her to see, then drop them in a wooden box.

"Drop. Listen, Mary Ellen. *D—r—o—p.* Drop the marble in the box."

"*Dra, dra, dra.*" Mary Ellen struggled to form the word. "*Dra, dra, dra.*"

There were exercises to discriminate between various objects, and Joan smiled as she watched this dignified woman pull out a cardboard illustration depicting a breakfast table with stamp-sized pictures of food—pancakes, bacon and eggs, a bottle of syrup, and a cup of chocolate milk.

"Where's the chocolate milk, Mary Ellen? Where's the chocolate milk?"

Mary Ellen studied the card and reached for the pancakes.

"Is that the chocolate milk?" Beebe asked. "That's not the chocolate milk. Where's the chocolate milk?"

This time Mary Ellen picked up the right picture.

"Hand me the pancakes, Mary Ellen. The pancakes." Mary Ellen dropped the pancakes in Beebe's outstretched palm.

"Very good, Mary Ellen. Hand me the syrup."

Mary Ellen searched Beebe's face for a clue to the command. But there was none. Beebe's hand was cupped over her mouth to prevent Mary Ellen from lipreading. Beebe repeated the command. "Hand me the syrup, Mary Ellen." Mary Ellen continued to study the cardboard and finally picked up the right card.

Beebe's children are required to speak, to use their memories, and to develop proper syntax. Discipline and persistence tie it together. Beebe demanded Mary Ellen's attention for an hour, snapping her out of daydreams, scolding her for sloppiness, praising her for good work. The sessions frequently seemed endless, wearing, frustrating. Joan watched and wondered if Mary Ellen would ever be the person Joan wanted her to be.

"What color is the dog?" Beebe asked.

Mary Ellen mumbled.

"What color is the dog?"

Mary Ellen mumbled again.

"I asked you a question," Beebe said. "What color is the dog?"

Mary Ellen's attention wandered.

"Listen to me, Mary Ellen," Beebe said, her voice firm. "What color is the dog? Is it yellow? What color is it? Is it yellow?"

Mary Ellen continued to mumble.

"You're not paying attention, Mary Ellen. You're going to stay here until you tell me the color of the dog."

"*Bla, bla.*"

"What's that *bla, bla*? I want to know the color of the dog."

The words ran through Joan's mind as she drove home with Mary Ellen, crushed by the torturous demands she made on her three-year-old daughter. Was it worth it? Would she ever learn to speak? Would she ever be normal? Joan wanted to cry. If only she could let Mary Ellen be a child, to be free and happy the way a little girl should be. But Joan couldn't allow it; that would mean throwing away Mary Ellen's life. Joan was struggling to free her daughter from a prison of silence, but she didn't have the key. She would have to claw through the walls until Mary Ellen was finally released.

It was becoming difficult to tear Mary Ellen away from her friends every Monday and Friday when she had a lesson with Beebe. What child would want to give up play, submit to being washed and dressed, and then be required to perform like an adult before therapists who demanded perfection? Home was like a nursery school for Mary Ellen with Mike and Kathy and many of the kids from the block. There was always something going on.

"Mary Ellen and her girl friends marched in the cellar with Halloween masks and flag," Joan recorded in her diary. Joan joined in and tried to get Mary Ellen to say the word "parade." She opened up the basement to all the kids and it became a child's fantasy world. This was the best way to teach Mary Ellen language. Joan had an antique organ in one corner and several boxes of discarded dancing costumes a friend had thrown out. Aunt Marge had contributed a basketful of her old clothes, shirts, blouses, and shoes. The children dressed up and pretended to be dancers and fairy queens.

One afternoon Joan and Grandmother Kennedy noticed that Mary Ellen and her friend Julie suddenly became unusually quiet in the basement. Julie was an inseparable friend who, like most children that age, never paid attention to Mary Ellen's deafness. She wanted to be a marine biologist when she grew up, and through Julie, Mary Ellen acquired an interest in insects and animals.

"I'd better go downstairs and see why it's so quiet," Joan said as she started down the basement stairs. The playroom was dark. She called out, and though they didn't reply she could hear them breathing.

"Mary Ellen, what are you doing?"

Joan was startled. Mary Ellen and Julie were hanging from the organ bench, their heads nearly touching the floor and their legs tucked over the bench. Each child was wrapped in one of Aunt Marge's old skirts that hung loosly around them.

"We're playing at being bats," Julie replied.

The children played games, tested the old organ, hid in

corners, in boxes. Mike played the organ's base pipes and his sisters and their friends ran screaming from the playroom.

"The Hemouth is coming," Mike bellowed. "The Hemouth is coming."

The Hubers' house became a favorite spot for the neighborhood kids and some even forgot to go home at the appointed hour. The Hubers had just seated themselves at the dinner table one evening when they heard faint cries coming from below. "What could that be?" Joan asked Dick. She rose and went to the basement stairs. Coming up from the dark was one of Mary Ellen's playmates.

The work continued. "Concentrating on discipline," Joan wrote in the diary. "Since Mary Ellen has been sick she's really gotten out of control. I'm making her use 'please' more often."

Discipline was the glue that would hold Mary Ellen together and force her to develop her hearing and acquire language. Beebe had succeeded before with other children and was determined to do it with Mary Ellen.

Joan and Beebe had discussed the need for discipline, and there wasn't a family enrolled at the clinic that didn't know Beebe's philosophy.

"Deaf children have more problems and are more difficult at the age of two and three," Beebe told Joan. "It's easy for a parent to give in, but that's asking for trouble. Deaf children are perfect con artists. They'll hoodwink you and try to take advantage of their hearing loss."

Beebe remembered a little deaf boy she had tutored in her last years in San Francisco. It was like breaking a wild horse. There was no way she could start instruction until she had him under her thumb, and it took months. But she succeeded.

"Beebe's tough, thank God she's tough," Joan told Grandmother. That Kennedy intuition told Joan that discipline was essential for all children. But not all mothers at the clinic felt as Joan did. Some complained because Beebe was not averse to using such old-fashioned methods as a spanking to control an unruly student, or a dash of water in the face to stop a tantrum. On a daily basis Beebe was very professional at the clinic.

But she had a tender side. It was evident in her patience, her humor with the children, and in her confidence that the children would succeed. Occasionally she revealed herself.

"You develop a certain hardness in teaching the deaf because you've got to be able to come out of a session and treat the next child. You can't have your emotional involvement carry over," she said to Joan.

Dr. Froeschels had warned her about becoming too involved with her children. He had seen her upset by the plight of a brain-damaged child and cautioned her, "If you're going to get yourself involved with every family you work with, you won't be effective."

Beebe's tough course did work. "Progress," Joan recorded in her diary. "Made apple pie today and at supper (with only one hearing aid working) Mary Ellen said 'apple pie.' It was nice and clear. We'll have to make more pies. Tried games with noisemakers using a whistle, harmonica, and a cooking pot. Mary Ellen didn't seem to hear the harmonica. We matched colors of spooled thread to the colors in her sunsuit, pink, blue, yellow. Mary Ellen repeated the colors and seems to understand and distinguish among them. She's done this before but always regressed or lost interest."

* * *

September 19. Today I drew a circle on the blackboard and Mary Ellen, with her back to me, put in eyes, nose, mouth, and hair after I asked her to do so.

September 20. Mary Ellen ran and got my comb when I told her to comb her hair. Progress! She put the comb away without a tussle before we went downstairs. She seemed to understand when I said it was time for cereal. She picked out the following animals in a book, bear, pussycat, doggie, birdie, and fish.

September 28. We're making nice progress with the storybook. Mary Ellen likes to get up and snuggle at your side. She understands now that I'm in charge of the book. She lets me do all the page turning.

October 1. Guffie says Mary Ellen seems to grasp the story she read to her. I'm to hold up on my stories until Beebe and Guffie lay the groundwork.

12

THE PROGRESS WAS AGONIZINGLY slow, but Joan believed she was on the right track and now knew she wasn't alone. There were other mothers with the same fears, hopes, and expectations.

One of those mothers was Claire Davis, whose son David was Mary Ellen's age and had been in therapy for over two years. Claire was a sharp-featured strawberry blond, an avid supporter of Beebe's method who was eager to help Joan whenever she needed guidance. Claire had shadowed Beebe when David was an infant, seeking all the advice she could get, and she knew how important the same support would be for Joan. The "old" mothers also volunteered their time to initiate the new ones, and Joan soon learned of Claire's story. It was familiar, though Claire had been lucky to have had a physician who was prepared for deafness and who knew that Beebe could offer help.

Joan and Claire met frequently in the clinic when both David and Mary Ellen were in therapy, and for Joan these sessions were her own form of therapy. They were like an opiate, fascinating and compelling. She could listen for hours without being bored. Claire's story was similar to Joan's and it began at the clinic.

David was still an infant when Claire carried him there, silently and nervously. When she and her husband stepped into the waiting room, they were momentarily distracted by the presence of the woman who greeted them. It was Guffie, who had virtually lost the use of her legs to polio when she was a teenager, and she maneuvered only with difficulty. A handsome woman with black hair and a soft reassuring voice, Guffie struggled into the waiting room, bracing herself in the doorway. Beebe was away in New York with Dr. Froeschels, so Guffie conducted the hearing test. She led them into the small therapy room with a bank of narrow rectangular windows high on the west wall. Jim pulled out a chair from a table under the windows, and Claire sat down with David on her lap. Guffie picked up a rectangular box and eased herself into a chair behind Claire. There was silence as she opened the lid, revealing several dozen small, oblong objects resembling wooden blocks. Each was an Urbantschitsch whistle, the same kind Dr. Froeschels had used to test Mardie almost twenty years earlier. If the patient showed no response, either by turning toward the sound or showing some kind of body reaction, such as the blink of an eye, a length of rubber surgical hose was attached to the whistle and the tone was blown directly into the ear. The whistles were compound tones, more comparable to speech sounds than the pure tones of an audiometer.

David wriggled in Claire's lap while Guffie leaned forward, blowing each whistle behind his ear, first the left, then the right. There seemed no response so Guffie attached the hose and ear olive and inserted it into David's ear. Still there was nothing. On the surface Claire seemed composed in her white and black checked suit. But underneath she was terrified.

"I was prepared for it," she told Joan. "But I was praying I wouldn't lose control because there was just no response from David, absolutely nothing."

"You must have been aware that David had a problem," Joan said.

"Oh, yes!" Claire replied. "We were aware that deafness could be caused by rubella. Our doctor was very alert to the possibility of deafness and he also was acquainted with Beebe and Mardie. He knew what could be done so he made arrangements to have David tested by Beebe. I don't think most doctors are aware of the alternatives to sign language or the need for a quick diagnosis."

Joan smiled. "Isn't that the truth?" she said.

Guffie worked with the quickness of a professional. Once she noticed a faint change in David's expression.

"He heard that one," she said. There was a tenuous link to the world around David, and Claire clutched her infant son and dabbed her eyes. But Claire and Jim knew there was no hope. Quietly they left, their world ready to collapse. They returned home to the large white house on College Hill and lay on the bed to weep. Claire remembers hearing the children playing in the street, reminding her of her childhood. She sobbed when she thought of David growing up on the same block.

Claire had been raised in another house overlooking the hills of Bucks County. When she and Jim were married they had returned to College Hill to live with Claire's parents. They liked the hill. It retained the flavor of simpler times, more like a village, where neighbors lingered to chat in the market, the drugstore, or on the street corner. The hill was crested by heavy woods. Below, the Delaware lumbered by and the latter-day Huck Finns swam in its clean and gently flowing currents.

Claire and Jim had their first child, Lisa, in 1957, and it wasn't until 1964 that Claire was expecting her second child. The pregnancy was well-timed. Lisa was in first grade, able to care for herself and to help with the baby. Claire and Jim were in their early thirties and Jim's career at the bank was progressing well.

After David was born on November 14, 1964, Claire and Jim tested him constantly during the first months. They would call out, clap their hands, and make loud noises outside his area of vision, hoping for some reflex that would indicate he heard. They looked for a jerk, a blink, a frown, a twitch. At times they were certain he heard and they grasped for any sign. They read up on the subject and devoured whatever literature they found. In the first months it was still too early to tell. They read that only after about three months does an infant begin to understand and respond to sound, and for sound to have meaning it must be loud enough to attract attention. After the first three months the child starts to locate the source of sound and he enjoys hearing his own voice and starts to babble and coo. Claire and Jim also read that some infants become so accustomed to sound they ignore it, making it difficult to test for deafness by using reflex action alone.

"That's exactly what we were told," Joan said. "It was so exasperating to see that Mary Ellen just wasn't hearing anything and the doctors in Philadelphia said she was sophisticated to sound. It was as though they were describing an animal. We know how humans respond to loud sounds and yet they kept saying she was saturated by sound."

Claire and Jim were far from being unsuspecting parents and they had an alert doctor.

"We were never relaxed," Claire said. "We were absorbed in trying to determine if David could hear."

Slowly they realized that something was wrong, then became convinced David was deaf. He was a happy little baby, active and interested. But he wasn't responding to anything, the bangs, the claps, or the voices. There was just nothing to indicate that David was hearing.

In retrospect, Claire, like Joan, remembered one phenomenon, David's eyes. They were so quick and alert, they followed Jim and Claire's every movement, scanned their faces. It was troubling. Only later did they learn that David's eyes were a clue to his deafness. Deprived of all sound, he relied on his vision to read the world around him. Facial expressions and gestures told him what his hearing could not.

But Claire and Jim were lucky. By now they knew that most parents don't suspect their child is deaf for years, or that their suspicions are not taken seriously by doctors. The average age at which a deaf child is diagnosed is 2.7 years, only a few months older than Mary Ellen when she was diagnosed. The Davises waited only four and a half months before seeking the answer they dreaded.

"I want you to take David to see Helen Beebe," Claire's doctor told her. He had just completed another examination of David and his conclusion was the same as Claire's and Jim's.

"Helen Beebe! But she's not a doctor," Claire protested.

She remembered being a grade school student and passing Beebe's small clinic on Cattell Street. Beebe and Guffie were crammed into the two small rooms that had once been a shoemaker's shop. Claire knew vaguely, like everyone else on College Hill, that Beebe worked with speech problems. But no one associated her with deaf children in those early days. "Mrs. Beebe's a speech pathologist!" Claire exclaimed.

"Claire, at this point no doctor is going to help you or be able to tell you anything more than Mrs. Beebe. She's worked with deaf children for years. She'll determine the extent of David's problem and if he is deaf, you'll be in better hands with Beebe than any medical specialist. She knows much more about it and can recommend a course of action."

He picked up the phone and called the Beebe clinic while David wiggled on Claire's lap. The doctor spoke briefly, then turned to Claire. "Can you go up to the clinic today?" Surprised, Claire nodded.

It was that afternoon that Claire and Jim visited the clinic and met Guffie. The results of David's test weren't the only blow that day. A teenage boy who attended a nearby residential school for the deaf stopped by to visit Beebe. Guffie chatted with him in Beebe's absence and he spoke in the breathy, nasal, sometimes rasping accent of the deaf who have barely learned to speak. Later, as Guffie blew each whistle, Claire saw her dreams for her son vanishing. She visualized David growing up, institutionalized, and using the same distorted speech as the young visitor. He was the specter of David in the future, Claire's nightmare come true. Guffie spoke to the boy, and they conversed and laughed. But Guffie was accustomed to his manner of speech, his alien tongue. She had become familiar with it through the years and was at ease with its strange sounds and intonations. Claire and Jim could not understand a word the boy said.

"If only Beebe had been there," Claire said. "She would have told us that you can't teach a child speech and hearing in a residential school classroom filled with other deaf kids. You can't expect a deaf child to imitate his peers when they, too, speak as poorly. You can't force a child to use his hearing by stimulating it an hour or so each day. Beebe had been through it all. She knew these schools and knew they were hopeless."

Joan could feel the despair in Claire's voice as she told her story. Claire and Jim went home from the clinic that day mourning the infant Claire held in her arms and the hopelessness of his future. They knew nothing about deafness, nothing about alternatives, or where to turn. They began making plans. They would move to Philadelphia where David could at least learn sign language and finger spelling. These seemed preferable methods of communication to the distorted language they had heard that afternoon. Depression settled over the Davises as it does over most parents when they discover their child is deaf. Both would be leaving their lifelong home, relatives, friends, familiar faces and places.

Claire and Jim returned to the clinic several days later to meet Beebe. They entered the waiting room and sat down. It was a strange encounter for Claire. She had seen Beebe countless times, in her clinic or walking to and from her large house several blocks away. Still, she was unprepared for Beebe's looming presence, the height, the confidence. "I really thought she would tell us about finger spelling and sign language," Claire said. "I had no idea she'd tell us David could learn to hear and speak."

Claire and Jim also were introduced to Marianne Derr, the same Marianne whom Joan had seen in her Catholic school uniform. Marianne had been undergoing therapy for five years, since she was four, and had missed those critical early years of language and hearing development. Nevertheless, her speech was good for a profoundly deaf child, and Claire and Jim reacted the way most people do when they meet one of Beebe's students, refusing to believe Marianne could be profoundly deaf. Her ability to hear and speak was electrifying.

"Beebe assured us David also could learn to talk and could be just like his normal contemporaries," Claire said. "And that afternoon when we got home, it was as if someone had given us a million dollars. If Marianne could learn to hear and speak, David could, too. He was only five months old and Marianne hadn't begun her therapy until she was four years old." Claire laughed. "Jim felt so good that day he went out and played golf."

13

JOAN REMEMBERED CLAIRE'S WORDS as she and Mary Ellen drove home. Some of the tension had drained because of her talk. She needed that support from other mothers who had been through it, even though Claire had told a tale of continuing struggle with as much despair as hope. David had been at Beebe's for more than two years, and the progress was clearly measurable. He spoke well, his vocabulary was rapidly expanding, and his hearing was developing. Still, the road ahead for Claire and Joan seemed endless, a journey of drudgery with a few moments here and there of elation. Joan remembered one of Claire's greatest moments, the day David heard his own voice for the first time.

It was a Saturday and Jim was off on an errand. Claire waved good-bye from the front door of their Raub Street home. She was on edge that day, but expectant too. Two weeks before David had received his first hearing aid, and Claire had carefully made a tiny vest, stitching in big pockets for the aids. She and Jim buttoned it around his chest, then ran the wire to his ear, gently inserting the ear mold. Claire thought he looked like a little old hard-of-hearing man. She switched on the power and stood back.

There was nothing, no change of expression. They waited for something, some sign that he heard. Beebe had warned them not to expect any change. "He just didn't hear anything," Claire told Joan.

Beebe was reassuring. "In time he will start to hear," she told Claire. "Give him time."

It had been two weeks and still Claire waited. She walked back from the front door toward David's playpen in the living room. It was time for his nap. Suddenly she stopped. Faint little sounds caught her ear they came again, *"ah, ah, ah,"* distant and cooing-like. Claire stood immobilized, the chills running down her back, not daring to move.

"Ah, ah ah." Claire knew David was hearing his voice for the first time. "I was afraid to put him up for his nap," she told Joan. "If I woke him he might not do it again." But the vocalizations continued. *"Ah, ah, ah,"* he babbled. *"Ah, ah, ah."* He said it when Claire came to get him in the morning and when they went out shopping. To Claire and Jim it was like a symphony reaching full crescendo. To others it was annoying. "Is that the only thing that child can say?" barked one man in the supermarket.

Beebe asked Claire to set up an appointment at a pediatric center in Philadelphia for a battery of tests. She wanted to know if David's hearing was his only problem or whether there were others that would distract from his therapy. Beebe had many deaf children who suffered from an assortment of disabilities. Blindness and hyperactivity were two that were common.

Joan imagined the trip to Philadelphia. Claire and Jim went down praying that the doctors might find that David wasn't profoundly deaf after all, that Beebe's diagnosis was mistaken. Maybe a simple operation could restore his hearing. But profound deafness was confirmed, and it was a turning point. Claire and Jim had no alternative but to accept David's condition though they were thankful the doctor found no other problem. He showed no response at most frequencies. "We were told that David couldn't even hear his own voice. A freight train rumbling by at 100 decibels would streak by silently. As far as his hearing conversation, it would be impossible without aids."

"Beebe was great," Claire told Joan. "She told me not to worry about the audiograms because he could still learn to use his hearing even with such a profound loss." And Claire and Jim were determined that David would succeed. The first time David heard his voice and vocalized was a catalyst. They knew they were getting through. They would start to build and eventually create an entire vocabulary, a language, a mind, and a personality from David's first babblings.

Joan remembered Claire's words. "Jim and I agreed that we would force David to hear or we would die trying. When it's your child, you'd be surprised how determined you can be."

Joan knew exactly what Claire meant. She listened intently as Claire told her of David's first months under Beebe's instruction. It wasn't new to Joan. It was the intensity of the program that dismayed her. How would she ever keep Mary Ellen's attention? But Joan had certain advantages. She was outgoing and talkative while Claire was shy and had to overcome a lifetime of reserve and introversion. The requirement that she keep talking to David took all Claire's determination. When she started she had no idea what to do.

"Talk to David, babble, make him hear the sounds he should be making for a five-month-old," Beebe said. "Babble, babble, and babble some more."

Even that was difficult for Claire. She had no way of knowing if David heard anything, and his lack of response made her acutely aware of his deafness.

She sat with David on her lap, forcing herself to make all kinds of baby sounds. Then she would stop momentarily, wondering who was listening. She laughed at her awkwardness and told Joan of how immune she had become to all the stares and curious looks when she talked to David in public. "It took me a while to be comfortable and so vocal around David," she said.

Beebe wouldn't accept David for therapy until he was at least a year old, a policy that changed as more and more rubella children showed up at the clinic. In 1965 David was the youngest child to whom she introduced her unisensory method, so-called because the deaf child is forced to acquire speech and language through one sense alone— hearing. Beebe would instruct Claire on what to do and Claire went home and worked with David. When Claire needed more instruction, she phoned Beebe or dropped by the clinic on a walk with David. Beebe would finish a therapy session and peek out into the waiting room to give Claire new instructions. Every Saturday Beebe stopped by the Davis house to observe the progress. From the beginning she was the master strategist who had the technical knowledge and who developed the overall plan for David's development. Claire and Jim were the tacticians on the front lines.

"Beebe made it plain that ninety-nine percent of David's instruction and development was up to Jim and myself," Claire said. "The remaining 1 percent was up to her. She was the counselor who would tell us what to do. We had to go out and do it."

Claire began her monologue with a small rubber ball, decorated on one side with a picture of a puppy and on the other with a rabbit, that squeaked when squeezed. She would hold it in front of David.

"Listen, David. Listen, David." She repeated the words incessantly, thousands of times.

"Listen, David. Do you hear the squeak? Hear the squeak. *L–i–s–t–e–n.*" For weeks there was no response. David would regard the ball, squeeze it, turn it over to point out the puppy and the bunny.

"See the bunny, David. See the bunny." Claire was on the floor on her hands and knees, speaking earnestly and loudly to her son. For fifteen minutes, for half an hour, for hours, she would use the same object, repeating its name. Maybe he would hear and someday say its name. Claire bought little bells and rang them close to David's ears.

"Listen, David. Listen to the bells. Bells."

Claire blew a whistle carved in the shape of a bird.

"See the bird, David. See the bird. *L–i–s–t–e–n.* Hear the bird, David. Hear the bird."

Claire banged on tambourines and triangles.

"*L–i–s–t–e–n* to the tambourine, David. *T–a–m–b–o–u–r–i–n–e.*"

The collection of toys grew. So did the multitude of sounds and noises. Claire's every action or chore was explained. She spoke to him when she changed his diaper in the morning, when she served him his breakfast.

"Milk, David. Drink your *m–i–l–k.* This is *c–e–r–e–a–l,* David. Eat your cereal. Egg, David. *E–g–g.*"

"If he was taking his bottle in my arms and looking up at the ceiling, I'd take advantage of the moment. See the light,

David, see the light. We'd switch it on and off. I'd walk into the kitchen and put him in his high chair. Look at the clock on the wall, David. Where's the clock on the wall? It's time for supper, David, where's the clock?"

Jim came home from the bank at lunch and picked up where Claire left off. "David, this is a sandwich. I'm eating my sandwich."

"What's this, David. David, look at this. *S–a–n–d–w–i–c–b.*"

"Cookie, David, this is a cookie."

Lunch ended and Jim would return to the bank and Claire would get down to David's level again, crawling along the floor with her infant son. They went into closets, explored the dark corners, studied the shoes and boots, and came out again to crawl past beds, chairs, sofas, under tables. All the time, Claire was talking, talking, talking.

When she went shopping she carefully enunciated the names of everything she bought.

"Chicken, David, chicken. Beans, David, these are beans." When she bought gas, she explained what she was doing. On walks she pointed out trees, cars, houses, people, dogs, cats. Jim came home again at night and relieved Claire while she made dinner. The ritual continued until bedtime. Jim gave David his bath, played with toys, and described them to him.

Claire would put David in his pram almost daily and wheel him down the steep grade of McCartney Street, talking to him all the way. People stopped at the odd sight of a woman talking to a toddler the way most people talk to an adult. "People looked at me and I'm sure they thought I was trying to create an Albert Einstein. But you have to take the time," Claire told Joan. "You can't talk baby talk to a deaf child who must learn to hear."

On their walks Claire and David turned up Monroe Street, past the drugstore and Jake's Luncheonette, to the small, one-story clinic. Claire wrestled David inside to wait for Beebe to finish a session. When she did, Claire asked her advice.

"When David first started therapy there were no other mothers with toddlers going through it," Claire told Joan. "But you have the benefit of a program with therapists and mothers who can give you the advice Beebe gave me. Beebe was constantly giving me reinforcement, encouragement, and ideas," Claire said. "You need that kind of support because no one fully understands the problems of raising a profoundly deaf child. Kathryn Derr was my only other source. She had experienced the same stuggle and endured the same pain."

Just to know if another child acted like David and had similar characteristics, was as stubborn or as funny, that was all Claire wanted to know. She found herself a pioneer, blazing the trail. Where she went astray, she and Jim had to backtrack and find the path. They realized that they alone were David's link to a normal life. With the exception of Beebe, no one else could help.

From the first babbles on a Saturday morning, David began making steady progress, though breakthroughs were measured in months, not days. David would appear to be absorbing so much, then would lapse and show no understanding of the information Claire and Jim had so diligently crammed into his head.

"David knew his name," Claire told Joan. "But if he called out 'mama, mama,' and I didn't immediately look up and into his eyes he would start saying 'David, David.' He knew that he responded when I called out his name. I used to wonder if he understood anything at all. I can smile about it now, but at the time it wasn't very funny."

David's development was good, largely because the therapy began so early. His development fell somewhere between that of the normal hearing child and the deaf child. The task for Claire and Jim was to pour in as many words as his mind could absorb. Most children are exposed to a flood of words every day. David was exposed to a trickle and he heard them only when Claire and Jim repeated them over and over. They had to ignore their fears and carry on. It was just before his first birthday that David spoke his first word. Claire and he were together in the bedroom cleaning out the closet.

"Ha," David said in a quiet little voice, his arm extended and finger pointing into the closet. *"Ha."*

Claire looked at David, her eyes following the line from his finger into the closet.

"Ha, ha!" David exclaimed loudly.

"What is it?" Claire picked him up and walked into the closet.

"Ha, ha." David pointed upward to a shelf above the closet where Claire kept her hats.

"Hats, David. Hats!" Claire shouted. David giggled and smiled broadly. "Hooray, David, you've just said your first word." Claire twirled in delight while David giggled more loudly. *"H–a–t, H–a–t,"* Claire emphasized. *"Ha,"* David repeated.

When Jim returned that evening, David was ready to perform. *"Ha,"* he said. *"Ha."* Claire, Jim, and David's sister, Lisa, stood around to applaud.

Other words soon followed. "Bye-bye," and later "daddy." David was at the threshold. Claire and Jim might be the only ones who understood him at this point, but David was using words.

"When he spoke those first words, I remember how delighted we all were," Claire told Joan. "Yet we were so overwhelmed at the same time," Claire recalled. "It was mindboggling to think this was just the beginning and so many more words would have to follow."

14

JOAN TRIED NOT TO think of the effort required to force Mary Ellen to use her hearing and develop language. Beebe encouraged and prodded. Joan listened quietly, her countenance camouflaging the rising sense of panic within.

"How am I going to do the laundry, the shopping, make the dinner, and all the other things I must do?" she secretly asked Beebe. Then she pulled herself together. It could be done, a little at a time, step by step. She wouldn't let the vastness of the task overwhelm her.

As a volunteer mother, that's what she told the new mothers coming into the program. Usually Joan volunteered the same days Mary Ellen was in therapy. She sat down with a bright-eyed, frightened young woman who was just as lost and confused as Joan had been when she first came to Beebe. How easy it would have been to discourage the new families.

"I'm cramming fifteen years into one home visit with you," Joan warned the new mothers. But she was quick to counter that all the home therapy could be incorporated in the day's activity. Mothers got up with their deaf children, made breakfast with them, did the dishes with them, the laundry, the cleaning, the shopping, the lunch, the dinner, and everything else that went into a day. At night when dad came home he became the teacher while playing with the child. If there were other children in the family, they too joined in. Still, trying to absorb the method was like trying to comprehend the meaning of life. If Joan thought about it at length, it became overpowering. She would take it word by word, fragmented sentence by fragmented sentence. She would make it her life. That was her job.

Joan's diary reflected the slow progress with Mary Ellen.

October 1. I've noticed Mary Ellen takes the following commands consistently in our morning routine: Get the comb; Get the brush; Get the pillows; Hang up pajamas; Put on panties; Put on shoes and socks; Put on overalls; Turn on the light; Turn off the light. Very little mix-up lately, but Mary Ellen still confuses hand and hair.

October 2. Good news from Guffie—Mary Ellen responded to commands without hearing aids. Guffie feels Mary Ellen definitely has been hearing more than we were told.

That really was good news. Joan always dreamed of the day she would take Mary Ellen to Philadelphia and the doctor would find that her unaided hearing had improved. It wasn't beyond the realm of possibility. Even Beebe was aware that a variety of conditions could influence the results of an audiometer test. She'd written about it in one of her books and Joan went over those words. "It is well known that there are numerous factors such as fatigue, general physical condition, emotional status, including cooperation of the patient, which can influence the audiometric result in a single case. Even for older children and adults audiometric differences of from 5 to 10 decibels seem to be physiologic."

Joan imagined coming home to Grandmother Kennedy and Dick screaming with delight that Mary Ellen's loss had diminished. What a day it would be. When Joan daydreamed like this she almost believed it had happened.

It was a false hope. Joan and Mary Ellen made the yearly trip to the hearing clinic either in Philadelphia or Harrisburg for a thorough examination. It was a day-long sojourn, and Mary Ellen was put through a battery of tests. This time Joan was expectant, hoping that Guffie's observation showed Mary Ellen's hearing had improved. But the tests revealed that the loss was just as profound as it had always been. Once again, Joan had to accept the reality that Mary Ellen's hearing would never be like that of a normal person and that no deaf child or adult with a severe-to-profound hearing loss would ever be able to use the unaided ear to hear much more than a few words. Deaf people with losses as great as Mary Ellen's live in silence without their aids. To Joan it would be like living in an underground cave. Mary Ellen, like David, was unable to hear her own voice or the steady, lub-dub of her heart. Most conversation is heard in the 55 decibel range. A whisper is about 20 decibels and a shout is about 80. With a loss of more than 80 decibels in her left ear and 110 in the right, Mary Ellen, at best, might occasionally be able to pick up a shout. If she were learning to respond to Guffie's commands without the benefit of her hearing aids, it was a clear sign that she was developing her residual hearing.

October 7. Mary Ellen had her back to the television when Pixanne (a TV personality) signed off. Pixanne said 'bye' and Mary Ellen turned and waved to her saying, 'bye.'

October 10. Mary Ellen sat and looked at a farm book. On one page she never raised her head and I asked where is the boy—the girl—mama—daddy—dolly? She pointed out each one. I know she didn't anticipate what I was going to say because I mixed them up.

October 12. Mary Ellen is getting the idea of sentences. She is piecing together more words. Now she says, 'thank you, mama,' or whoever it happens to be. She says, 'milk, please,' 'orange juice, please,' or whatever it is she is demanding.

October 13. Worked on the concept of hot and cold water again. For a while I thought she had caught the meaning, but now I have my doubts.

Concepts are hard to teach even to a normal child, but normal children hear them every day without interference. Joan had to inject them into Mary Ellen's mind: hot, cold, warm, cool, dark, light, high, low, and on and on.

"Where do I start?" she ruefully asked Dick one evening after the children had gone to bed. He had learned to read how well the day had gone when he set foot in the door in the evening. It wasn't only the difficulty of teaching Mary Ellen that was taking its toll on Joan. Kathy and Mike needed attention, too. Mike was still the wiry, active kid he'd always been and Kathy was beginning to show signs of resenting all the attention Joan had to devote to Mary Ellen. Joan was determined to give as much to her other two children as she could. She had to show all the misguided professionals, particularly the therapist from the Children's Society, that she could do it all. By the end of the day, though, she was frequently near tears.

"It never ends," Joan told Dick. "Sometimes the thought of another ten years of dealing with a deaf child is overwhelming. I just don't know if I can do it. God never told me how difficult it would be. He knew if He told me I might have quit."

Joan smiled, trying to forget the frustration. She knew she'd never quit. It was against her nature.

Time off for worn-out mothers was an essential ingredient in Beebe's therapy. Frequently Beebe approached Joan after a therapy session.

"And what is mother doing for herself this week?" she asked. Beebe knew that if the mother burned out, the child would never succeed. The mother's health was almost more important than the child's, and the clinic published credos to follow so that the mother was always able to teach another day. Every new mother enrolling her child in the clinic received a copy of A Mother's Pledge, adopted by Sally Farr, Chairman of the Voice for Hearing Impaired Children in Toronto, Canada:

(1) I accept that more than anything else I care about the future of my hearing impaired child.

(2) I accept the fact that nobody else is going to do the necessary work or make the necessary effort for me. I MUST do it myself.

(3) I accept the fact that it is going to be difficult, perhaps the most difficult thing I have ever had to do.

(4) I will seek help wherever and from whomever I need it; be it educational guidance, psychiatric

counseling, audiological and medical advice or support from other parents. I will not be over-awed by professionals; their services are available to help me.

(5) I will not let any "if onlys" get in my way. "If only I didn't have younger children; if only I were wealthy; if only I had live-in help; if only I didn't have to work; if only my husband understood; if only my child had a little more hearing," etc.

(6) I will not dwell unduly on the sacrifices which I am making.

(7) I will always remember that any procrastination on my part now will threaten the future of my child.

(8) I will organize my day in order to give myself some time of complete privacy.

(9) I will work hard and consistently and take a regular holiday.

(10) I will have a good cry and ventilate my feelings without feeling ashamed.

Likewise the fathers had their own pledge, this one also adopted from the Canadian Hearing Society:

(1) Do not complain if the house is not perfectly neat and tidy. In the first couple of years of auditory training, mothers find themselves with little time for serious housework. When you are trying to take advantage of every opportunity for teaching your child, routine and organization are often impossible.

(2) Be a good listener when mother feels like talking about a problem and be sympathetic when she feels like crying.

(3) Give mother a break (even if it is only for twenty minutes) by playing with or entertaining the children when you get home from work. She desperately needs this, particularly if the hearing impaired child is an only child and she has been alone with him all day.

(4) Encourage her to get a baby-sitter to provide time, not only so she can get out by herself but also so that the two of you can regularly get out alone together, away from the child. Occasionally, a weekend baby-sitting exchange can be arranged with friends to give the two of you a chance to get away alone.

(5) Participate enthusiastically in auditory training games.

(6) Remember which words the child is learning in lessons each week and try to reinforce these casually as much as possible.

(7) Be enthusiastic about the child's progress, no matter how slow, to make mother feel her efforts are worthwhile.

15

JOAN PUSHED ON WITH concepts. She made Mary Ellen feel the water temperature, demonstrated dark and light, used the ceiling and the floor to show up and down. Mary Ellen stared incomprehensibly. Joan persisted and developed her own teaching tools. She took a sock and filled it with objects that Mary Ellen knew, a tiny doll, a block, a ball.

"What's in the sock, Mary Ellen?" Joan asked. "*Feel* the sock, Mary Ellen, *feel* the sock. The doll is *inside* the sock, Mary Ellen, the doll is *inside* the sock."

Joan removed the object from the sock and placed it in various places around the kitchen. "The doll is *under* the table, Mary Ellen, the doll is *under* the table. The doll is *on* the table, Mary Ellen, the doll is *on* the table."

Joan took the toy doll and placed it high on the window frame next to the kitchen table. "The doll is *above* the table, Mary Ellen, the doll is *above* the table."

The lessons went on day after day with limited success. Joan could tell Mike and Kathy to "hit the road" every night at bedtime. They knew what it meant, but for Mary Ellen such phrases only brought a look of confusion.

Concepts weren't the most important aspects of acquiring language at that point in Mary Ellen's life. Her vocabulary still was limited compared to her contemporaries, and her articulation was such that others frequently had difficulty understanding what she was saying.

October 17. We get "OK" or "all right" from Mary Ellen when she does something. All right is clearly spoken but I'm the only one who knows it's OK, but that's OK.

Joan was aware that Mary Ellen had many of the strange vocalizations of the deaf, a nasal quality that made her sound as though she had a cleft palate. She seemed to swallow words, and anyone unaccustomed to her speech found it difficult to understand. Beebe warned mothers not to worry. Their children's language development was still in the primitive stages. Time would improve it. They would progress well beyond stilted speech and many would eventually talk with only a slight accent. Joan was amused by Mary Ellen's manner of speech. She was beginning to sound like a gangster; *dese* and *dose* instead of *these* and *those.* Mary Ellen couldn't hear the subtle sound of the *T.* She would never really hear high-frequency sounds like *T, S,* and *Z.* Through years of training, though, Beebe's students would learn to reconstruct those sounds.

Mary Ellen was turning out to be a singer and most of her repertoire consisted of church hymns learned every Sunday. Joan was amused by her musical daughter. Mary Ellen's favorite place to perform was on the potty. Joan would plop her down and the Hubers were frequently serenaded by a faint soprano voice that wavered from the upstairs bathroom. Who would have predicted a few years earlier that Mary Ellen would even be able to carry a tune?

The alphabet also was a challenge. Mary Ellen was proud when she recited it: *A, B, C, Ddddddddddddd.* She could only distinguish the first three letters.

Beebe wasn't concerned. There were so many aspects of language to be mastered. Articulation would develop as Mary Ellen grew older. Beebe was striving for fluent speech and knew it would come. It was better for Mary Ellen to develop a good vocabulary and string these words into reasonably well-articulated sentences than to pronounce words artificially in sentences that no one could understand.

Everyone took a turn teaching Mary Ellen. During the day Grandmother Kennedy frequently worked with her. Joan pasted several calenders on the kitchen wall, and Grandmother Kennedy taught Mary Ellen the days of the week, birthdays, or religious holidays. She and Joan worked hardest trying to teach the concept of day and night, summer and winter. Most difficult was trying to instill an understanding that summer weather still lingered when fall arrived and that winter often lasted well into spring.

Grandmother Kennedy was Joan's greatest helper. If she couldn't stay, she poked her head in the door to say hello. She was more than Joan's mother, she was her best friend and confidante, and Joan often wondered how she would cope without her.

Grandmother Kennedy usually cared for Mike and Kathy when Joan and Mary Ellen drove to the clinic. Joan had her hands full on those days. Just corralling Mary Ellen and dressing her for the trip to Easton took a day's energy. Joan frequently chased Mary Ellen around the house, wrestled her into her good clothes, and plunked her in the car while

Mary Ellen raged and screamed. Joan didn't want to count the times she got behind the wheel in despair. Where and when would it end?

When they returned, Mike and Kathy were always scrubbed clean, ready to visit Aunt Marge in Emmaus, south of Allentown. Aunt Marge lived near a park with swings and slides and always served soda and pretzels, forbidden treats at home. The kids adored Aunt Marge. Joan called her the gypsy of the McDonald girls, so pretty and large, warm and outgoing. Grandmother Kennedy was slight, reserved, and conservative compared to her younger sister. Aunt Marge always wore colorful, flowing skirts and was bedecked with jewelry that clanked when she tussled with the kids. Grandmother Kennedy, in contrast, wore simple, clean-cut chino skirts and Ivy League shirts and never had a hair out of place. Joan took after her mother.

The hour after dinner was the usual time when all the Hubers joined in to teach Mary Ellen and the sessions became ritual.

Teaching was Joan's solitary effort in the mornings and afternoons, and the house and the world were the classroom. Other family members were encouraged to help with Mary Ellen and at times the lessons took on a carnival atmosphere. One evening after dinner, Joan lined up the family in the living room, Dick, Mike, Kathy, and Mary Ellen, to do calisthenics. The objective was to show Mary Ellen how to follow instruction.

"All right, now," Joan said. "We'll start with jumping jacks. Ready. One, two, three, four . . ."

The living room shook, vases, ashtrays, memorabilia jangled as arms, legs, and feet flailed the air.

"One, two, three, four. One, two, three, four." Joan joined the line of jumping Hubers bouncing up and down in the living room. Joan and Dick were laughing at themselves, and the kids were enjoying it, too. Joan glanced over her shoulder and stopped suddenly. Not all in the Huber family were partaking in the exercises. Mary Ellen had found a nice spot on the couch, and was looking intently at the pictures in a magazine.

Frequently they gathered around the circular table in the pine-paneled alcove off the kitchen where Joan did her teaching. They played games, tested Mary Ellen with flash cards, and worked on her elocution. Dick was amused one night when the game involved blowing a Ping-Pong ball around the kitchen table. It was Beebe's invention, designed to improve Mary Ellen's pronunciation of the letter *P.* Joan and Dick got down on their knees, their heads just protruding above the surface while the kids stood. Joan started the game off, placing the ball in front of her mouth and blowing—*PPew.* The ball skidded across the table toward Dick. *PPew.* It shot toward Kathy. *PPew.*

"Listen to that sound, Mary Ellen," Joan said. "Listen to the *P,* the *PPew* whenever it's blown. The *PPew* as in *P.*"

PPew, PPew, PPew, for half an hour. Kathy was particularly active in Mary Ellen's therapy. She visited the clinic at times and was allowed to watch Beebe or Guffie working with Mary Ellen. Beebe encouraged these visits to acquaint Kathy with the instruction. It was endless repetition of what seemed like the most simple things. But Kathy got the knack of it. Occasionally she mimicked Joan while she worked with Mary Ellen, and Mary Ellen responded by pelting Kathy with crayons.

October 18. Kathy helped me put Mary Ellen through her paces. They did the following commands:

Look out the window; close the door; open the door; turn on the light; turn off the light; sit on the bed.

A few days later Joan was concentrating on colors again.

October 21. Worked with plastic cars, red, yellow, blue, green. On request, Mary Ellen handed me the correct colors. Green still is a bit shaky, but I think she's mastered the others.

October 22. While I was sewing she pointed to some orange piping I was using and told me "orange?" Also, if she says "one, two," I say "three," then she says "four, five." Numbers are a bit complicated, but they are coming.

October 23. Mary Ellen made her first attempt to say, "You're welcome."

October 25. Mary Ellen has started asking constantly, "Where is the comb?" "Where is the pussycat?" "Where are your shoes?" She says these every day and it's constant.

October 26. I thought Mary Ellen said "It's broken," showing us a broken toy. If she said it once, she'll say it again. We played the game Candyland, much to our astonishment.

November 1. Now we can say, smile, laugh, cry to Mary Ellen and she understands. She also dances to Grandmother's song "New Shoes," and bows on command.

November 3. Mary Ellen has picked up Kathy's favorite word, "watch." She says, "Watch, Mama," then performs some trick.

November 6. Mary Ellen has picked up Beebe's and Guffie's favorite word, "Listen." Tells us to listen when on the potty, so we do.

"Listen" was the word Mary Ellen heard most during therapy. Beebe or Guffie frequently began a sentence with, "Listen, Mary Ellen, listen." Mary Ellen also picked up other traits from the clinic. She began speaking with her hand cupped over her mouth, mimicking the therapists. Joan was amused, knowing that Mary Ellen assumed this was the way people spoke to each other. After all, Beebe was the great master teacher and if she did it, it was correct.

Joan also laughed at Mary Ellen's inquisitiveness.

"And how old are you?" Mary Ellen asked visitors to the Huber household. "What is your name?" These were questions Beebe and Guffie asked all their children. As she grew older and was able to converse with greater ease, she asked more questions and sometimes drove Kathy crazy. "What's that?" "What's this?" "Why?" "What for?" "How do you know?" But Joan recognized that Mary Ellen's outgoing personality was born out of her need to communicate, and she was reluctant to change this behavior, even though it frequently meant that visitors were put through a short and embarrassing interrogation.

Joan and Grandmother Kennedy laughed at Mary Ellen's antics, the laughter releasing some of Joan's anger and frustration. Mary Ellen was becoming stubborn and strong-willed. Kathy and Mike could be just as difficult. But when Joan laid down the law to them, they obeyed because they understood. If she attempted to discipline Mary Ellen, the child sometimes flew into a rage. It was a struggle to get her to Beebe's, to communicate the need for therapy, to get her to work at home without constant badgering. The trips down Route 22 to Easton were becoming a chore, with Mary Ellen sulking in the backseat of the Hubers' long station wagon.

"I practically have to bind and gag her," Joan told Grandmother Kennedy. The first few miles were fine, but beyond that Mary Ellen started to scream and squirm from her seat and jump into the back of the wagon. Once they reached the clinic, Mary Ellen was the perfect little lady, polite and agreeable, going quietly into the therapy room. She knew Beebe took no nonsense. If Mary Ellen misbehaved, Beebe disciplined her and sometimes left the room.

"She's being naughty and I told her she'd stay in there until she behaved. Do you have time to wait?" Beebe asked Joan, who was in the waiting room. Joan always had time and was thankful Beebe was so demanding. It was the only way Mary Ellen would succeed. She knew Mary Ellen was afraid of Beebe, whose gray eyes could subdue recalcitrant children with one icy stare.

Yet Joan frequently gasped from the pity and sorrow she felt for her youngest daughter. She would never know how deeply Mary Ellen suffered because of her deafness, how much of her personality would be shaped, or warped, because of the handicap. Dick in particular was gripped by watching Mary Ellen around children her own age. They jabbered in delight while Mary Ellen remained silent, unable to pick up their conversation. In winter it was even more difficult for her to hear. Sweaters and heavy coats covered her aids, which were fastened in pockets on her chest. All sound was muffled. She was a trouper, though, never complaining, seldom crying. She would cut her finger, stub her toe, scratch her forehead without uttering a sound. She would march into the house, ask for a Band-Aid, and then disappear to play again.

"I wish, I wish, I wish it never had to be," Joan said to Grandmother Kennedy. But she knew what her mother would say, just as she would say of the adversity Grandmother Kennedy had seen in her own life with Grandma McDonald. It was God's will. She would abide by it. But sometimes it seemed so harsh.

"God sent me only what I can bear, nothing more, nothing less," Joan said. "I must grieve, but I've got to figure some way out through God's grace. This is my trial, my cross. But He gave me the strength to get this little girl through. If I fail, I fail myself, and more importantly, I fail Mary Ellen—she will be the loser."

16

Despite the frustrations, Joan found great satisfaction in teaching Mary Ellen. It wasn't the job of most mothers who worked with normal children. Their task was to put together the pieces of a puzzle. Joan started with nothing, an absolute blank, and she not only had to put the pieces together; she had to construct them all before they would fit. Joan could stand back and marvel at the progress she had achieved. When she considered the prognosis for most deaf children, Mary Ellen was a miracle.

"It's just so fascinating to watch Mary Ellen develop," Joan said to Grandmother Kennedy. "To think you can take this child, and against all odds make her talk and hear. It's amazing." Occasionally, Joan's diary reflected the excitement and challenge of seeing Mary Ellen succeed. She was still only three.

November 9. Big Thrill!! Mary Ellen heard the phone for the first time. We didn't have the bell turned up and never realized it. We also let her listen to the phone

124

through the mike. It never ocurred to us before (I'll never understand why) to let her listen to the phone. She heard Grandmother Kennedy and got very excited and ran around looking for Grandmother. Grandmother said pussycat and Mary Ellen repeated it over the phone. There's no mistake. She heard it.

November 12. Mary Ellen says John and Judy now. Color getting more accurate. She hardly ever misses on yellow and orange. Counts to five easily and fairly accurately. Counts everything. GOOD, GOOD, GOOD!

November 13. Got new telephone receiver. Mary Ellen definitely hears from it but isn't as interested as we expected. It has encouraged her to react to the ring of the phone, though. So in time I'm sure she'll be interested in chatting on the phone.

November 15. Mary Ellen says "wake up," as plain as can be!!

November 19. Guffie sent home cards she says Mary Ellen works well with. They depict colors, objects, and numbers. I had no success with them, though. Of course the noise level in the house was high. Not a quiet corner to be found. I'll try again when Mike and Kathy aren't around.

December 4. Christmas is approaching and Mary Ellen is well versed in Santa Claus, Ho-Ho-Ho, Christmas tree, snow, which she calls *"ugh,"* and pretty snow, which she calls *"ugh-ugh!"* We've also been picking out "Happy Birthday" on the piano. She enjoys this and seems to recognize the tune.

December 10. Mary Ellen has the Nativity down pat, i.e. Baby Jesus, Mary, and Joseph.

December 18. Candles in our windows and now Mary Ellen understands the word candles. She's gone from calling them happy birthdays to candles. Pronounces them *"andles,"* and it's hard to distinguish her word candle from her word for angle.

December 23. Mary Ellen's vocabulary takes another spurt—Christmas tree, Christmas card, pretty tree, Frosty Snowman, pronounced *"noman,"* Christmas lights, and Christmas star.

December 28. Social outings and Christmas were a real boon to Mary Ellen's vocabulary and understanding. She's taken to asking "Who's that?" when a new face comes in our door. She has a little trouble remembering new names, but makes a fair attempt at it. A new game called Lite Brite has really planted colors firmly in her vocabulary. We even throw in a wrong color to her and she corrects us. Mixes purple and blue sometimes. Her colors are red, yellow, blue, green, orange, pink, black, purple, brown, and white.

December 29. Pasted pictures of big bird, little bird, big ball, little ball in the bathroom. Every morning Kathy points to the correct object as I question her. Then Mary Ellen is eager to follow. At night Mike takes his turn. I feel if we do this consistently, she will catch on to opposites. Her speech is really sloppy. I guess since we've been out socially with her I notice it more.

Beebe was noticing, too. She picked up on the deficiencies of all her children and knew the remedy: more hard work and even tighter discipline. Joan was in full agreement, but knew Mary Ellen would retaliate somehow. Week in, week out that winter, Beebe put Mary Ellen through her paces, demanding, cajoling, forcing, even laughing on the sly at the antics of this self-willed little girl. Mary Ellen was so naughty, yet lovable, as she squared off against the no-non-sense professional who demanded she learn the basic sounds of speech.

"Repeat after me, Mary Ellen," Beebe demanded. *"Ba, Ba, Ba."*

"Ba, Ba, Ba," Mary Ellen mimicked.

"Good, Mary Ellen. Now this one. *Boe, Me, Doe."*

"Bow, be, doe."

"Boe, me, doe," Beebe repeated.

"Bow, be, doe."

"You're not listening, Mary Ellen. Now let's get it right. *Boe, Me, Doe."*

"Bow, be, doe."

"You'll repeat it till you get it right," Beebe warned as she shifted in her chair. *"Boe, Me, Doe."*

Mary Ellen's head was down in a sulking position. She didn't respond immediately and seemed to ponder a reply. *"Boe, Me, Doe,"* she said.

"See, you can get it right," Beebe said. "Now let's try some more.

"Ca, Ca, Ca. That's an easy one," Beebe said.

"Ta, Ta, Ta."

"No, Mary Ellen. It's *Ca, Ca, Ca."*

"Ca, Ca, Ca," Mary Ellen said.

"Good, Mary Ellen," Beebe said.

Joan peeked briefly through the small glass window in the therapy room and could tell by the way Mary Ellen held herself that she was fighting Beebe all the way. Joan was puzzled by the growing rebellion, hoping she could find a way around it. Yet she sympathized with Mary Ellen. What normal person could stand to repeat simple phrase after simple phrase day after day, week after week, year after year? Mary Ellen was a bright child, just as easily bored as another. Joan also knew that Mary Ellen realized that she had to stick with it to learn to communicate. Even so, *ba, ba, ba, ca, ca, ca, boe, me, doe*—who wouldn't be ready to scream?

The rebellion wasn't without its humorous side. Joan remembered the "Little Indian" days when Mary Ellen pretended to talk by constant babbling. The Little Indian became "Polly Parrot" who repeated everything said to her and then laughed with mischievous glee.

"How are you, Mary Ellen?" Joan would ask.

"How are you, Mary Ellen?" came the reply.

"No, no, Mary Ellen. You say 'fine' when I ask you how you are."

"Fine."

"Mary Ellen!"

"Mary Ellen!" She laughed happily and danced around the floor.

Joan persisted. "What's your name, Mary Ellen?"

"What's your name?" Mary Ellen replied.

"No, no. Your name is Mary Ellen, *Mary Ellen.*"

"Mary Ellen, Mary Ellen."

Joan was caught between amusement and frustration. She never knew when Mary Ellen couldn't understand or couldn't hear and when she was just being playful. Joan had a plan. She would use Kathy to respond to the questions first and then ask Mary Ellen to repeat what Kathy had said. That had always worked in the past and it should work again. She put Kathy and Mary Ellen side by side in the kitchen.

"Now, Mary Ellen, I'm going to ask Kathy some questions and I want you to listen. I want you to repeat what Kathy says. Understand? Let's try it."

"What is your name?"

"Kathy."

Joan clapped and cheered the way she always did with Mary Ellen when she got a right answer. "Hurrah!" Joan shouted. She turned to Mary Ellen.

"What's your name?"

A broad smile broke over Mary Ellen's face, and she began to giggle. Joan was smiling broadly too, hoping Mary Ellen would respond with her own name.

"*K–a–t–h–y,*" Mary Ellen said slowly.

Joan managed a slight smile, but she soon turned serious. She had to win this round or Mary Ellen might decide to play the game forever.

"What's your name?" Joan repeated over and over. Mary Ellen's mischievousness began to fade when she realized Joan would stand in the kitchen until she responded correctly.

January 2. Mary Ellen is going through a bad period of freshness! I'm finally getting through to her despite screaming and bucking me. I won't budge until she asks for things nicely. Sometimes it takes half an hour for her to get what she wants and sometimes she doesn't get what she wants because she refuses to be nice. Once or twice now she has condescended to take back her screaming and ask nicely. Till this period is over, *I'm* going to be deaf.

"Me go to Grandma's!"

"You can't go to Grandma's today, Mary Ellen," Joan said. "You know we're going to Beebe's." Joan realized how much Mary Ellen wanted to be with Mike and Kathy at Grandmother Kennedy's house. Grandmother took them shopping and gave them soda and ice cream while Mary Ellen was shut in with Beebe, repeating words, sounds, identifying animal noises or pictures in a book. There was no way Joan could explain to Mary Ellen that her life depended on regular therapy sessions with Beebe. Monday and Friday seemed always to produce this pathetic ritual of Mary Ellen begging to be with Grandmother and Joan having to pack her in the car.

"No, no, no go," Mary Ellen cried as Joan prepared her for the trip. She dashed off into the upstairs or down to the basement to hide. Joan gave chase, and pulled her screaming to her room, where Joan struggled to make her presentable.

"We'll stop at Jake's on the way back and have a milkshake," Joan promised as she peeled off Mary Ellen's play smock and put her in her best dress. Jake's was the luncheonette across the street from Beebe's, a gathering spot for clinic parents and their children. Jake and his wife knew the Beebe children and always spoke to them cupping a hand over their mouths.

"Chocolate," Mary Ellen demanded.

"OK, chocolate," Joan agreed as she combed Mary Ellen's hair.

"I don't like promising her treats all the time," Joan confided to Grandmother Kennedy.

"Just be careful not to let it get out of hand. You could spoil her that way," Grandmother cautioned.

"I worry about that," Joan admitted. "But when you see what that poor child has to go through every week, I don't think we really give her enough credit for all she's doing. Mike and Kathy have a ball with you and Mary Ellen will always be deprived of that. If she didn't resist me, I'd wonder about her. I kind of admire her for all her spunk."

The tortuous trips down Route 22 continued. Mary Ellen screamed all the way to the clinic and was mischievous as only she knew how to be. Joan seethed at one incident in Grandfather Kennedy's car. Mary Ellen had been so well behaved that Joan knew she should have been on guard. Mary

Ellen carried her own lunch of coveted jelly sandwiches. No one noticed anything unusual until Grandfather Kennedy picked up several fellow steelworkers, and one bellowed from the backseat.

"Hey, Kennedy, what the hell are all these jelly sandwiches doing stuck to the back window?"

"Oooh," Joan uttered and gritted her teeth when she heard the news. There would have to be retribution. It meant that the next trip down Route 22 would be even more difficult, but Joan was determined to discipline Mary Ellen. She armed herself with a flyswatter with which to threaten Mary Ellen when she misbehaved. There was no other way to enforce discipline on the road except to stop. Mary Ellen was too sly. She screamed and carried on just beyond Joan's reach and the flyswatter seemed the answer. It worked temporarily. Then Mary Ellen took to jumping into the rear of the station wagon where she thought she was safe. She was until the day Joan had had enough and pulled over to the shoulder, turned off the engine, and crawled over the front seat, then the back seat, her skirt riding up. She later wondered what the truckers thought as they drove by.

In the far reaches of the car Mary Ellen was equally surprised as she saw Joan crawling toward her. No bribe that day either.

At home the lessons continued.

January 3. Amusing thing happened. I said something to Mary Ellen and she said, "What?" Really caught me off guard and I broke up completely.

January 8. Mary Ellen understands and says, "Hold your sleeve," a very practical phrase for dressing. Also understands "Hold up your chin," but she doesn't attempt to say this phrase. We're still having trouble with comparisons, big and little.

January 9. Last night we played hide-and-seek with various sized farm animals, a big cow, a little cow, a big horse, and a little horse. Mary Ellen seemed to understand the differences. Sometimes I can't tell if she's teasing or whether she doesn't understand. She never points to the correct picture for big bird, little bird, big ball. I suspect she's faking it.

January 11. Going back to our grab bag. This time we will put in big and little combs, brushes, cows and horses. Maybe the old trick will help her catch on.

January 12. Tonight at supper Mary Ellen asked as clear as a bell, "Where is the butter?" We were stunned.

January 19. Mary Ellen had a good telephone conversation with Grandmother Kennedy. Answered to: "What's your name?" "How are you?" Recited Jack and Jill (after a fashion). Also Mary Ellen has started recognizing her written name. I suspect it's guess-work, but it's the start.

January 28. Mary Ellen's vocabulary has expanded with descriptive adjectives: nice, pretty, lovely. She understands these words all mean the same thing. We're happy about this because it proves to us not only her vocabulary but her comprehension is expanding.

January 31. Today, after months of my telling Kathy her record player was too loud, Mary Ellen got up, covered her ears, and said "too loud Kathy," and turned down the record player.

Joan was aware that Kathy and Mike could easily feel left out because of the time she spent with Mary Ellen. During the summer, on holidays, even weekends, when Mike and Kathy were not in school, Joan worked with Mary Ellen. At night the family games really were designed to help Mary Ellen.

"You spend almost an hour with Mary Ellen every afternoon after lunch," Kathy complained. It was a barb for which Joan was prepared, but just as it was difficult to explain to Mary Ellen why she had to take therapy twice a week, it was hard to tell Kathy why Mary Ellen required special tutoring every day. She looked into Kathy's pleading and wondering little chubby face.

"And you get to go to Grandmother's all the time when Mary Ellen has to go over to Beebe's. Don't forget that. You know that Mary Ellen is deaf and requires a great deal of attention so that someday she can hear. You can hear everything in the world. Just think if you couldn't hear the birds or the television. What do you think that would be like? But Mary Ellen can't hear any of that. That's why I have to spend so much time with her. Kathy, don't mix up attention and love. True, I give Mary Ellen more attention because she needs it and you don't. But I love you and Michael just as much as I love Mary Ellen. It would be *impossible* for me not to love you all equally!"

No amount of explanation seemed to change Kathy's feelings. She and Mike didn't perceive Mary Ellen as being deaf. They didn't understand it. She was just their bratty kid sister, who required too much attention from Mom and Dad and always was making a nuisance of herself.

Kathy persisted in her complaints about Mary Ellen, demanding to know why Mary Ellen was always the first to be put to bed at night. The three kids gathered in Mary Ellen's room at bedtime and Joan read to them. When the first reading was over, Mary Ellen was tucked in and they moved to Kathy's room. When Kathy was under the covers, Joan took Mike to his room and read to him for a few minutes.

"But you always read to Mary Ellen first. Why don't you read to Mike and me first and Mary Ellen last?" Kathy whimpered. Joan tried to explain that Mary Ellen was the youngest and had to go to bed first. But Kathy wanted to be first.

That night Joan read first to Kathy. She gathered all the children in Kathy's room and they sat next to her on the bed. She opened the book and began to read. Mike and Kathy were absorbed in the story, their faces intent with interest. It was about an elephant who sat on an egg until it hatched and the baby bird emerged with a trunk as well as wings. The kids especially love the pictures.

Mary Ellen wasn't interested. She listened for a minute, then began jumping up and down on the bed.

"Sit down, Mary Ellen," Joan warned.

But Mary Ellen continued to bounce.

"Mary Ellen, you must either sit down and listen or you will go to bed immediately," Joan said.

Mary Ellen paid no attention. Joan dropped the book and marched Mary Ellen into her bedroom and tucked her into bed. She returned and continued reading. When she finished, it was time to take Mike into his room. Joan tucked in the covers of Kathy's bed and bent down to kiss her.

"Tomorrow, let's go back to reading to Mary Ellen first," Kathy whispered. "I think it's better that way."

17

It was easier for Mike to accept the family's concern for Mary Ellen. The less attention his mother paid to him, the happier he was. Dick was a Boy Scout Master, and Mike was always in tow at scout meetings and outings where his little sister was well out of mind. During the summer, the troop frequently went on camping trips in the densely wooded and deep green Pocono Mountains, whose ridges appeared from Allentown like the spiky backs of sleeping dragons. Mike was the mascot, proud and strutting with his Mantle-Maris hat that seemed to be sewn to his head. Whenever Joan spoke to him it seemed she was speaking only to his nose. His eyes remained hidden beneath the cap's bill. The only time it came off was when he went to bed, and Joan was amused by the different colors of his face, bronzed by the sun from the forehead down.

For Mary Ellen and Joan the work continued at the clinic and Joan grabbed whatever time she could with Beebe to review Mary Ellen's progress. She knew Beebe was impressed with Mary Ellen's language capabilities, but it was for that reason that Beebe urged Mary Ellen on to greater heights.

"You must enroll her in a nursery school this fall," Beebe told Joan. "Mainstreaming is one of our most important goals, to educate the hearing-impaired child to live comfortably in the normal world."

"Do you have any schools in mind?" Joan asked.

"No," Beebe said. "The more typical the school, the better. The object is to expose Mary Ellen to normal speech and language." Beebe picked up a book and leafed through the pages until she found the passage she was looking for. "We adhere to this admonition," she said and read a brief sentence. "'If you don't ever segregate, you won't have to worry about integrating.' When I was teaching the deaf back in the 1930s, they were all segregated and their speech was just awful. Of course we didn't have hearing aids in those days, but the children had never been exposed to normal speech. And some of them with less severe hearing loss might have been able to pick up relatively normal speech by being around their hearing peers."

Joan mentioned the disciplinary problems she was having with Mary Ellen, the freshness, the back talk, and the trips to the clinic. "She's fine most of the time when she's here," Joan said.

Beebe laughed. "That's because she's afraid of us. You'll just have to clamp down. You know how I feel about discipline. You can't start letting her get away with things. Discipline for parents of the deaf is naturally going to be more difficult. You have guilt to deal with, remorse and fear that other parents don't have. The child knows that and will take advantage of you if you let her, and then you might as well forget all the therapy because it won't work."

Joan knew how tough Beebe could be on parents. She had seen her scold them in the waiting room after or before a therapy session. She remembered one mother who picked up her child and began to carry her into the therapy room.

"Put her down," Beebe said. "She's quite capable of walking. You should let her walk from now on; otherwise she'll expect you to carry her wherever you go."

Beebe disappeared with the child, and the mother looked hurt as she sat with Joan in the waiting room. The woman shook her head half in exasperation, half in amusement. "She's never had her own children," she said. "If she had, she'd know that after a day of dealing with a three-year-old, things go a lot faster if I carry her. Otherwise it takes so much time to do anything."

Joan laughed. "Poor Beebe," she thought. "It's easy to criticize her. Parents don't like being scolded and the kids can't stand the therapy. But without her the children and parents would be lost."

Joan knew Beebe's tough veneer, but she'd also heard stories from other mothers that revealed the kindness and warmth of this woman who sometimes appeared so distant and aloof.

Everyone had heard the story of Glenny and Beebe. Glenny, too, had been born a rubella baby, scarred by the epidemic of 1964. But the disease struck him with devastating effect. He was born profoundly deaf, with a heart defect, and was later diagnosed as hyperactive. If Joan thought her plight was tough, Glenny's mother faced a Herculean effort every day. As a two-year-old, Glenny needed open-heart surgery and doctors labored throughout one night to save his life at a Philadelphia children's hospital. Beebe kept her own vigil that night, calling Glenny's mother's every hour for reports on the operation.

Joan also knew about one of Beebe's students who had asked God to restore her hearing.

"Why did I have to be born deaf?" the girl asked Beebe. It was a question Beebe frequently heard, but this time it was particularly poignant because she told Beebe God had not responded to her prayers.

"Sometimes there are things in life that we can't do anything about," Beebe said quietly. "Not even God will help at times."

Beebe told the child of her own life, and how she had been married and hoped to have her own children. That was many years ago and now it was too late. "Why was I never able to have children?" Beebe asked. "You must live with your deafness and I must live with the sorrow that I was never a mother."

Joan remembered the first time Mary Ellen asked why she was deaf. It was a hot day and Joan was undressing her for bed. She peeled off Mary Ellen's shirt, revealing the straps that supported her hearing aids. Mary Ellen had begged to wear a halter like her sister and all the other little girls on the block. Joan bought one and tried it out, but it wouldn't support the weight of the aids.

"When do I stop wearing earrings?" she asked.

Joan thought for a moment, trying to tell Mary Ellen as gently as possible. "You'll have to wear them all your life," she replied.

"Why?"

"Your friend Julie wears glasses and she can't see without them. She'll have to wear glasses all her life, too."

Mary Ellen listened as she sat on a tabletop next to the window. Joan waited for more questions. But Mary Ellen seemed to accept her mother's word. She pointed to a bird in the tree outside her bedroom window. "Birdie," she said.

Joan stood and walked over to the therapy room and glanced through the small window to observe Mary Ellen and Beebe. It was amusing. Beebe's jaw was moving back and forth and she was making strange sounds. Joan had heard Beebe mention her "chewing therapy," but had never seen it in use. Like discipline, it was a tenet of Beebe's philosophy.

"I learned the chewing method from Dr. Froeschels," Beebe said afterward as Joan readied Mary Ellen for the trip home. "It's something Mary Ellen must learn to do. It will give her better pitch and full resonance." Beebe handed Joan an article she had written that explained the chewing method. "Keep it. I've got more," she said.

Joan worked her way through the technical language that night to understand the concept of chewing therapy. It was unique to Beebe's method. Years ago Dr. Froeschels concluded that speaking movements were similar to those used in eating. He theorized that if patients with speech and voice problems pretended to chew food while they spoke it would improve the tonal quality of their voice. He knew the deaf couldn't hear their own voices, so they couldn't control the tone as a hearing person could. The voices of the deaf frequently lack harmony and are shrill, making their speech incomprehensible. "This can be changed by vocalized chewing," Beebe wrote.

Joan learned the chewing method and applied it in her instruction. She continued pouring in the words, hoping they stuck in Mary Ellen's mind. Joan had seen statistics that frightened and depressed her, and realized there was no way for Mary Ellen to keep abreast of a normal child. Joan had to do the best she could. A normal child between the ages of three and six learns five and six hundred words a year and goes to school with a vocabulary of two thousand words. By the time most children are fourteen, they have learned between eight and ten thousand words.

Joan despaired at the thought of ever expanding Mary Ellen's vocabulary by that much. But she kept on despite Mary Ellen's resistance.

April 4. Puzzled? Judy, our four-year-old neighbor, brought a talking toy over that is the same kind that Mary Ellen once had. When Mary Ellen had hers, we were disappointed because she didn't seem to hear it. Today she wouldn't put Judy's toy down and it's perfectly clear she could hear it. Again I wonder how much Mary Ellen is fooling us. Hopefully she is.

April 5. First preschool reading class was a success. Librarian said Mary Ellen more readily participated than Kathy. We both laughed. I had predicted this because of Mary Ellen's outgoing personality. She learned new words also. Today, after leaving the clinic, we parked near the Lehigh River in Easton. Mary Ellen said, "Look—water." I said that's the river and she repeated perfectly clearly—"river." She also caught onto the word naughty being the same as bad. It was a big day!

April 16. Without fail, Mary Ellen can read Mama, Daddy, Mary Ellen, Michael, and Kathleen. I am going to print the names on new papers to see if she is just accustomed to seeing the same words on the same paper or whether she really can read these words.

May 9. Mary Ellen points out one and two objects to me, one girl, two boys, etc. She correctly answers the questions, "Who is your brother?" "Who is your sister?" Her vocabulary grows every day, but her speech is still sloppy. I'm hopeful this is impatience and not the best she can do. We've also started playing a new game, Memory, which she enjoys and understands.

Mary Ellen's ability to recall facts and figures was remarkable. Joan took flash cards depicting various objects and turned them over. Mary Ellen remembered every one. It was a terrific way to teach vocabulary since Mary Ellen would learn the name of the object on each card. She loved playing the game and soon even Joan was unable to win. Mothers of other deaf children had noticed the same memory capability in their children; it seemed to be characteristic of the deaf.

18

JOAN NEVER EXPECTED DIFFICULTY in placing Mary Ellen in nursery school, but she decided to enroll her immediately before classes were filled. Joan called the YWCA nursery school and explained Mary Ellen's deafness.

"I'm sorry, Mrs. Huber, but it's our policy not to accept handicapped children," the administrator told Joan.

It was another blow. Joan realized how insulated she had become. She accepted Mary Ellen's handicap. Others did not.

Joan was angered and hurt by the rejection. Her mother noticed.

"It's probably just as well the Y didn't accept Mary Ellen," Grandmother Kennedy said. "They wouldn't have been able to deal with her needs."

Joan felt the same frustration that had dogged her before she found Beebe. The woman at the Y had politely said Mary Ellen could not keep up academically with normal children.

"Oh, phooey," Joan ranted to her mother. "Mary Ellen is just as able to keep up as any of those children. Her vocabulary is not as good, but her mind is just as bright and she probably knows a lot more than most of them."

The Y wasn't the only school that refused to take Mary Ellen because she was deaf. Another placed Mary Ellen on the waiting list, and Joan knew the staff had no intention of accepting her.

Joan suffered when Mary Ellen was rejected. It was something that shattered Dick, too. Both Joan and Dick had seen Mary Ellen's anguish when she couldn't follow a conversation or when other children wouldn't let her play because she was deaf. Then there was that woman down the street.

"Oh, she was so stupid," Joan said to Grandmother Kennedy one afternoon. "And she's a college graduate and a trained nurse. You'd think she'd have more sense."

The woman held a birthday party for her daughter, and both Mary Ellen and Kathy were invited. It wasn't long after the party began that the woman appeared at the Hubers' doorstep holding Mary Ellen's hand.

"Is there something the matter?" Joan asked as she came to the front door.

"I don't know," the woman said. "I think she may want to go potty."

"Didn't she say potty?" Joan asked.

"Well, I wasn't sure she knew what potty meant," the woman replied.

"She knows what it means," Joan said almost curtly. "When she goes potty, I'll bring her back."

"Oh, good," the woman said without enthusiasm. "We'll be there another hour or so."

Five minutes later Joan walked Mary Ellen up the street, trying to control her anger. She wanted to ignore the entire incident and keep Mary Ellen home until the party was over, but she couldn't be too proud for Mary Ellen. It would hap-

143

pen again until Mary Ellen was able to take care of herself. Joan knocked on the door.

"I've brought Mary Ellen back."

"Won't you stay?"

"No, I have things to do." Joan returned to the party after completing her errands and waited on the curb until it was over.

"We'll show all those stupid people," Joan said to Dick that night. He knew when Joan needed to talk. He also new she was more hurt than angered. It hurt him, too, to listen to the sufferings of Mary Ellen and Joan, or any of his children. His voice was quiet, deep, and level, which helped calm Joan when she was upset. He would sit in the kitchen, his face showing little emotion, his dark eyes seemingly unperturbed. And the flecks of gray in his nearly black hair made him look older, less like the very young man Joan had first met.

"Try not to let incidents like the birthday party upset you, Joan," Dick said. "They're going to happen all her life."

"Why do people have to be like that? I wanted to hit her for being so ignorant. She should know better than to treat someone like that."

Dick felt the instinctive desire to join in Joan's condemnation of their neighbor, but knew that would only aggravate the anger and the pain of seeing Mary Ellen rejected. He couldn't carry on effectively at home or in the office if he was filled with emotion and hostility. Mary Ellen had made progress since Joan and Beebe had been teaching her language and speech. But it was progress measured against a different set of standards. For a deaf child, she was remarkable in her ability to use her hearing and to speak. But most people, unaccustomed to her speech, had a hard time understanding her. Joan had to concentrate on the future when Mary Ellen would speak like a normal child, through Beebe, hard work, and the grace of God.

"Let's not dwell too much on the birthday party," Dick said. "Let's keep trying to get Mary Ellen in a good nursery school. That's the most important thing, and I'm sure we can do it. There are plenty of schools around."

Joan soon had Mary Ellen enrolled at a nearby Presbyterian Church in Bethlehem where the teacher, though apprehensive, expressed an interest in working with a deaf child. Joan drove over with Mary Ellen to meet the teacher and explain how well Mary Ellen could comprehend and take instruction. School didn't start for several months, but Joan wanted to be prepared.

May 10. *A B C* are planted firmly in Mary Ellen's vocabulary. She recognizes them on request. But . . . we can go no further because she says *C* like *D*. Until we're over that obstacle I don't feel it would be wise to go on.

May 20. We were out riding with Mary Ellen. I thought she was saying flower. But she kept saying "no flower" and getting angrier if I would repeat flower. Suddenly I realized we had passed a church and she was blessing herself—"In the name of the Father."

May 25. Finally got Dr. Seuss's *The Cat in the Hat Beginner Book Dictionary*. Wonderful book. All children enjoy leafing through it. Decided I would ask same three questions over and over again until Mary Ellen gets the idea what I want, i.e., (1) Count them or how many?; (2) What is _____ doing? (3) What is that?

May 26. Mary Ellen loves to go to our shopping center. She knows the names and says Almart (nice),

Grants (nice) and Food Fair (dirty). The reason for the nice and dirty is that she knows there isn't any toy department in Food Fair. In Grants we have a nice waitress interested in Mary Ellen and we let her order her own lunch when our friend is working. Lunch is usually hamburger and "purple," which means grape juice. Now when I'm fussy I make her say grape soda, but not too often because our waitress friend gets a bang out of purple.

May 27. New words . . . descriptive, i.e. finished, fix it, hole, all gone. Fix it replaces a grunt and pointing. Hole replaces broken. Also she picked up the words "Help! Help!" from the "Lassie" TV program and she uses them correctly.

May 28. Discouraged . . . all family relationships—brother, sister, uncle, father, mother, grandfather, grandmother—down the drain. Mary Ellen has either forgotten, is confused by it, or is just sick to death of it. She enjoys teasing, too. Asked her this morning, "Who is your father, Mary Ellen?" She said "Kathy," and roared with laughter. I'm dropping the subject for a while.

The burn-out syndrome was familiar. Joan knew that the demands placed on Mary Ellen were greater than on other children her age. The instruction and pressure were constant at home and the clinic, and Mary Ellen could not go on without some side effects. Joan would ease off at times, as would Beebe. But they knew that Mary Ellen's future depended on getting right back to the grind after a few days.

May 29. Played riddle game with Mary Ellen and Mike and Kathy. Drew a blank from all sides with no results.

Joan needed Grandmother Kennedy as never before. "Mary Ellen's regressing," Joan said tearfully over her coffee. "She just seems to be sliding backward. And I'm terrified this effort really is for nothing. I live in fear that all those people who said Mary Ellen would never make it are right after all, and the whole thing with Beebe has been a dream."

"You know it's not," Grandmother Kennedy spoke forcefully.

"It's so hard, Mom, so hard. Every day is a struggle. Taking her to Beebe's is like packing a wildcat off to the zoo. And I have to fight off these doubts. Sometimes I wonder whether I can cope."

"She'll make it," Grandmother Kennedy said.

"She will, but I won't," Joan laughed.

May 30. Got new numbers book. Mary Ellen loves it. Today she recognizes the numbers 1, 2, and 3. Tomorrow who knows? While watching a TV program the other night, she stunned Grandfather Kennedy by pointing out there were five girls singing and one boy. She held up her fingers and said: "Five little girls, one boy." Yippee!!

June 2. Another ray of light peeped through for me today. I let Mary Ellen out to play in Judy's sandbox.

June 3. Mary Ellen invited to another birthday party. She understood this time and knew where she was going and whose birthday it was. She signed her card for Alice and printed Alice on her envelope. On the way to the party she made sure the neighbors saw Kathy and her in their "pretty dresses."

June 4. We had supper at Grandmother Kennedy's. Grandmother got out little plastic dishes while we had our coffee. Mary Ellen pretended to fix us pizza pies, eggs, coffee with cream and sugar. For fun we acted up at the table and she scolded us when we were "naughty."

June 5. Mary Ellen read these names: Michael, Kathy, Mary Ellen, Mama, Daddy, Cat, Dog, Bunny. Grandmother, Grandfather, and Uncle Eddie are still a bit fuzzy.

19

BEEBE'S WAITING ROOM WAS where Joan took her own therapy, and when Claire Davis was waiting for David, Joan and Claire talked until the children were finished.

"Is David in nursery school yet?" Joan asked Claire.

"He started last fall," Claire said.

Joan was impressed by Claire and David. David was serious and docile compared to Mary Ellen, and was the clinic's stellar student. Teaching a deaf child seemed natural to Claire. But she laughed at such suggestions. David was a prince in Beebe's presence, but he had his moments. He might not have been as vocal about his objections to the clinic as Mary Ellen, but he disliked the therapy sessions nevertheless.

"We have David enrolled at the College Hill Presbyterian Church, just a few blocks from home," Claire said. "It's really convenient because Jim drops him off on his way to the bank and I pick him up around noon."

Joan listened as occasionally they could hear the sounds of therapy from the enclosed rooms.

"Has it helped him with his language?" Joan asked.

"Oh, yes!" Claire said. "I think one of the greatest satisfactions Jim and I have had from David's schooling is that he's learning from someone other than us. That was a real milestone when he came home one day and said something that we had not taught him. He learned it at school, and now we know he picks up things from the teacher and his classmates, not just his family."

A young mother entered the waiting room with a child about two, and Joan noticed the toddler looked odd with large ear molds and wires dangling down to the aids on the child's vest. Claire spoke up.

"When David went to nursery school I was very depressed by how far behind he was compared to his classmates. They were so vocal, and it took all that David had just to be understood. But you can't dwell on that. He is behind his contemporaries and will be for many years."

David was progressing, though. He too loved to sing, always off-key, but he managed a semblance of the melody. Each month the teachers used a different instructional motif, and in November the theme was Thanksgiving. The Davises hung pictures of turkeys around the house and talked about Thanksgiving and what it meant to Americans. At the nursery school, the children were taught about the Pilgrims, Indians, and the first days of the Massachusetts Bay Colony. They sang the traditional songs with the boys dressed in headdresses and the girls in bonnets.

Sometime before Thanksgiving, David began a little ritual that piqued Claire's interest. They would walk home, often taking a different route, crunching through leaves, observing and discussing nature. Claire was surprised as she rediscovered College Hill, where she had lived most of her life. With David she saw detail on houses she had never noticed before—cornices, doors, carvings—all crafted by artisans in the last century. Once home, David would disappear into his room. Claire hovered nearby, watching, puzzled, then amused. David took his child's chair and carefully placed it facing the side of the bed. He lifted the bedspread gently and folded it back. Then he sat down and with a flourish began. At first Claire was uncertain what he was doing until he began singing in his small soprano voice. He was playing an imaginary keyboard at the edge of the mattress.

"I will always cherish that moment," Claire said. "The words were all gobbledygook, but he was trying to sing a Thanksgiving song."

Claire listened each day until she caught a bit of the melody, then called one of David's teachers to ask for the words to the song. The next time he performed, she stepped into the room singing, "Over the river and through the woods, to Grandfather's house we go. . . ." When Lisa and Jim returned that night, the entire family joined in and sang the song in David's room.

"He learned to appreciate music in nursery school," Claire said. "And I'm sure it will be the same for Mary Ellen. So don't let anyone tell you the deaf can't enjoy music or even TV. David watches cartoons all the time."

"Do the teachers treat David any differently at nursery school than the other children?" Joan asked.

"Not at all," Claire replied. "After Mary Ellen's lesson, ask Beebe for the list of suggestions that parents can give a new teacher. It explains to the teacher that the deaf child is not to have preferential treatment except in seating. Teachers are asked to speak directly to the child and not to speak while facing the blackboard. David does everything the other children do. They all sit at tables and color, build with blocks, and sing. Then they all go down the hall to the recreation area and play. It's really so helpful. You know, the sooner you get Mary Ellen in a class, the better off everyone will be. For one, it will give you a little free time. And don't worry about Mary Ellen getting adjusted. I think you'll find that Beebe's children are better adjusted than many kids this age. So much is expected of them they're more mature except for their language skills."

"I've often thought that Mary Ellen is more outgoing than her sister Kathy because she's become so used to authority," Joan said. "She's been going toe-to-toe with authority since she started therapy at three years, and she's no longer intimidated by adults."

Claire laughed. "There are so many old wives' tales about the deaf not being well adjusted. I've got to tell you this story. One of the times that Jim and I took David to the children's hospital in Philadelphia, the doctors told us never to allow David to sleep without a night-light. They said that a deaf person waking up without light is like a normal person waking up with a pillow over his face. So we kept a light on for the last four years, and one night David asked why the light always stayed on. I didn't want to suggest that he would be scared in the dark, so I said that we were afraid he'd get up some night and stub his toe when he couldn't see where he was going. He thought for a while and then said he didn't need it and for us to turn it off."

Joan smiled. "I have Mary Ellen enrolled at a Presbyterian Church nursery school in Bethlehem, and I think it will be really helpful for someone else to be teaching her part of the day. I'm beginning to wonder if I'm getting through to her. She'll go along fine for a week, learn a new word or show understanding of a phrase or sentence, and then she'll just act as though it all leaked out."

Claire chuckled. "It happens to all of them. I remember

teaching David to say hello or good-bye to friends who came to the house. We'd go over what he should say and he would have it down pat. And he'd say the right thing when a friend came over. Then one day a friend was about to leave and I said, 'David, say bye-bye to Mrs. so-and-so.' He looked at me rather curiously and said, 'David, say bye-bye to Mrs. so-and-so.' I could have died. We'd spent so much time on that, and now he was only echoing without giving any thought to the words and the meaning."

The conversations with Claire were useful to Joan, who had tried many times to teach Mary Ellen with the same results. One day Mary Ellen appeared to have learned the lesson. The next it was forgotten and Joan went to bed depressed because the effort was just too great. She needed mothers like Claire to talk to, laugh with, and share her depression, fears, pride, and successes.

Beebe stepped out of the therapy room, followed by Mary Ellen. "I want you to work on those S's and TH's. She's not getting them."

Joan knew that Guffie had devised a method for teaching Mary Ellen to say S. The S is a high-frequency sound that many deaf children are unable to hear. But they can feel the pinpoint of air that rushes from between the teeth whenever S is pronounced. Joan took a common straw and held it vertically to her chin so that an end was next to her teeth. As she pronounced the letter, air was channeled down the straw for Mary Ellen to feel as it came out the bottom. Over and over Joan said S and held Mary Ellen's hand under the straw to feel the air.

At the clinic Beebe drilled Mary Ellen on S and TH and other sounds that she was unable to hear and pronounce.

"Ssssss," Beebe hissed. "Ssssss. Sssam."

"Tam," Mary Ellen replied.

"No, Mary Ellen. *Sssssam.*" Beebe took Mary Ellen's hand and placed it close to her mouth to feel the air from between the teeth. *"Sssssam, Sssssam, Sssssam."*

"Ttttttam, Ttttttam, Ttttttam," Mary Ellen replied.

There also were gains.

June 6. PROGRESS! Took a ride to see friends with a puppy dog. Mary Ellen was really taken by the dog. I said did you like the puppy dog? Mary Ellen repeated "puppy dog." I asked what was the doggy's name? Mary Ellen said "Freckles."**HOORAY**!!! First time she answered that question with no prompting.

Mary Ellen loved animals, dogs in particular. Nibbles, the vagabond who sometimes wandered by the Hubers' house, was her favorite. She entertained him until the day she followed him onto nearby railroad tracks. That was the last time Nibbles was welcome.

At Long Beach Island, New Jersey, where Joan and Dick took the kids for a week each summer, neighbors had two basset hounds that Mary Ellen befriended. They were the center of her world, and she announced her destination whenever she went to visit them. Joan never tried to correct her diction. It was too amusing.

"Mommy," Mary Ellen said. "I'm going to see the bastard hounds."

Joan and Dick made an effort to take trips with the kids during the summer. In addition to the week at the beach, there were fishing trips with Dick and a tour of the airport. Best of all were camping trips to the Poconos. They'd throw the camping gear in the car and take off to Hickory Run or the Delaware Water Gap. On arrival everyone unloaded as Joan cooked dinner. Afterward the kids roasted marshmallows over the campfire. On one outing, Joan set off to fetch some groceries at the corner store. She rounded a bend and was amazed to see a bear off to the side of the road reaching into a tree for food. To Joan it had to be at least eight to ten feet tall. Who would believe she ever saw a bear that big? Everybody knew Joan was a teller of tall tales.

Whenever the Hubers returned from a camping trip, the kids were scruffy and dirty and Joan and Dick tired. They had just pulled in one Sunday afternoon when Grandmother Kennedy called.

"Aunt Frances and Aunt Helen are over at my house, and Aunt Helen wants to see the children before she goes back to New York," Grandmother said.

"Oh, Mom, the kids are filthy."

"Well, I guess the only way she'll see them is dirty," Grandmother said.

Joan scrubbed them as quickly as possible and combed their hair. Mary Ellen sat down at the kitchen table with her new bug catcher that was filled with creatures of all varieties, one of them particularly hideous and eating all the others. Aunt Marge and Helen entered and approached Mary Ellen. Joan sensed their curiosity as they spoke to her, testing her hearing, waiting for her to speak.

"Want to see my bugs?" Mary Ellen asked.

"Of course," Aunt Helen said, thinking Mary Ellen would let her examine them through the glass. But, Mary Ellen calmly pulled off the top of the cage and overturned it on the kitchen table. Scores of insects and bugs scrambled away. From a distance Dick heard shrieking from the kitchen. Aunt Frances flew out the side door onto the patio. Aunt Helen charged into the corner of the kitchen. Trapped, she screamed in terror.

Life wasn't always this exciting.

June 10. Mary Ellen has taken another leap in many directions so far this summer. She says and understands the following: "I'm cold, accident, I don't want it, I don't like it, I like it, I'll fix it, I'll hold it." She knows everyone's name, some first and some last. Now we can tell her where we're going and she understands and gets excited. She also distinguishes between ocean, bay, and swimming pool. She knows tadpoles, frogs, chipmunks, spiders, mosquitos, mosquito bites, waterfalls, tunnels, squirrels. She knows her own age and the ages of her brother, sister and her friends: Mary Ellen 4, Kathy 5, Michael 7, and Judy 4. She has broken her toe and knows we went to the hospital to have a picture taken of it.

June 15. Mary Ellen is understanding more. She wants to go bye-bye all the time. Tonight Kathy went to have stitches out and Mary Ellen made a fuss when she spotted Kathy in going-away clothes, but she didn't want to go when we explained Kathy was going to the doctor. That was the end of the fuss.

June 19. Mary Ellen didn't want to take a nap today. But I explained after she napped we were going to a farm to see cows, chickens, ducks, pussycats, and puppy dogs. She went right in for a nap with no trouble so I know she understands what I said.

July 7. Mary Ellen now states her full name, says Grandfather Kennedy is fat, understands when I say we will do such and such before we do it. This is particularly helpful with things to eat. If she has candy she understands that first you eat lunch, then you get the candy. Today she pieced together a whopper of a sentence, "Look—pretty flower over there."

July 17. We're all busy recovering from Mary Ellen's third audiogram. We're disappointed but not quite as stunned as the last two times. Mary Ellen is in the profound class. The brighter side: the girl who tested her said Mary Ellen was beautifully trained (I wish that was the case at home). She said it didn't appear Mary Ellen had lost much despite her handicap and that she is practically on a par with a normal four-year-old. Hallelujah! Looking forward to next year. We were told to come back in one year for another audiogram. Already I have this last audiogram figured out. Mary Ellen was sleepy and didn't do her best listening. That'll keep me happy—so I'll believe it.

July 21. Started keeping a picture diary for Mary Ellen. This project will be very interesting for me because I feel I have also learned much in this year and can really watch and appreciate what Mary Ellen will grasp from her school book—a diary. We started the book April 28 on Grandfather Kennedy's birthday. I am concentrating on asking questions such as "What did Grandfather get for his birthday?" Until now I've had to point to the picture drawn and give her the answer so she could repeat it. But last night a rainbow appeared in the sky. Mary Ellen saw it and we quickly drew it in her book. She answered the following questions without prompting: What did you see tonight? Answer— a rainbow. Where did you see it? Answer—over there (*ober der*). Mary Ellen's finesse with getting acquainted has certainly improved. A man at the supermarket noticed her because he has a nine-year-old deaf grandson. He spoke to her and got good, clear, and correct answers. Man: Hello, how are you? What is your name? Mary Ellen: Hi. Fine. Mary Ellen. Four. While at the market she also made friends with a girl her age and learned the girl's name, Anita. Anita didn't seem to notice Mary Ellen's aids.

July 22. Mary Ellen pretended to call a friend on the telephone. We tried to coach her. She became indignant and told us "Shh! Sit down . . . stay there . . . drink coffee."

July 23. On the way home from Easton, Mary Ellen told Kathy, very clearly, "Get in the back!"

July 24. Tonight before bed we reviewed a very full and interesting day. I showed her a newspaper photograph of newly ordained priests we had met that day. She spontaneously said *Faver* for Father. Then she promptly went around and gave us all her blessing. She put hands on our heads, made us join hands, said mumble-mumble, and then shook our hands. I think Mary Ellen aspires to become the first lady priest.

July 25. Have noticed Mary Ellen answering pretty consistently to questions. Would you like some _____? Answer: Yes, please. What do you say? Answer: Thank you.

July 30. We had a very severe thunderstorm. It knocked all our lights out. Mary Ellen cupped her hands to her ears and said: "Wow. Tunder . . . too loud!" Also, her singing of "Happy Birthday" has definitely improved.

August 2. I saw Mary Ellen from the second floor and called to her to put down her stick. She looked up and around and found me. I repeated, "Put down the stick," and she did as she was told. I think I was more surprised to have her obey than the fact that she heard me.

August 3. Mary Ellen has taken to ignoring me. She has me concerned one minute because she seems not to hear me. Then the next she tells me "girl is sad," and I realize she recognized there is a girl singing on the radio and the song is sad. She also recognizes a happy song because she says, "girl better."

August 5. A question and answer with no prompting. Question: What did we have for dinner tonight? Answer: Spaghetti. Mary Ellen pronounces it *ba-detti.*

August 7. Mary Ellen plays the game, "Guess what I have" pretty well. Has the idea but, of course, can't give clues. She understands some clues and guesses correctly occasionally.

August 10. Mary Ellen played "What's in the box?" easily. We used only three objects. Next time we'll use four objects.

August 12. She is beginning to understand concepts of "on top of," "under," "over," "beside."

August 20. Mary Ellen went to our new public swimming pool. She ran around like a water sprite and was too brave for my comfort. She jumped right in. Luckily Dick was there and fished her out. She says "wimming pool," for swimming pool. This evening the sunset was unusually brilliant and cast a great shadow. New word for Mary Ellen, "shadow."

September arrived, and it was school time again. Joan was anxious about Mary Ellen's first year in nursery school. No

matter how good Mary Ellen's ability to speak and understand, Joan knew she was behind other children her age.
Nursery school would be the test. If she couldn't stay
abreast, what would Joan do? The prospect of the residential
school near Philadelphia kept coming to mind. Joan knew
more about these schools now. Groups of mothers and children from the Beebe clinic occasionally made trips to residential schools in the area. The contrast between Beebe's
children and those in the school was stark. Those children's
language was barely comprehensible. They spoke with their
hands moving quickly, rhythmically. They received instruction through signs and conversed with signs. Joan could
only thank God she and Mary Ellen had been spared.

Joan's other responsibilities kept her busy. Kathy and
Mike had to get to school every morning, and Mary Ellen
watched tearfully as they went off each day. Her nursery
school didn't start until the end of the month and until then,
Joan pressed on with the instruction. There were some improvements.

September 7. Noticed Mary Ellen using the adjective
"too" correctly. She's saying "I'm too hot" or "It's too
loud."

September 8. This morning I noticed Mary Ellen is
catching the word "went." She says, Daddy "went" to
church. Michael "went" to church. She used to run it
all together—*Daddywennachurch.*

September 15. Mary Ellen has been using the word
"mine" for some time. Today I noticed she has also acquired the words "you," and "yours," and uses them
correctly. I heard the words before but only when she
was repeating them in her Polly Parrot fashion. Today

she asked me: "My shirt?" I said, "no." Mary Ellen said, "your shirt?" I said, "yes." Mary Ellen said, "pretty . . . new."

September 19. Spoke with Mary Ellen's nursery school teacher last night. She impressed me as being a personality who would attract and keep Mary Ellen's attention. I also came home with a great deal of apprehension. Mary Ellen is just not capable, language-wise, of some of the nursery school activities. It was good to see what will be expected of her. I'm busily getting her ready for such things as show-and-tell, story time, and nap time.

20

NURSERY SCHOOL FOR MARY Ellen finally began, and Joan was pleased that she showed no fear when introduced to the class. Mary Ellen was proud to be going to school like her big brother and sister and mingled easily with her classmates and the teacher.

October 1. After two days of nursery school, Mary Ellen is in seventh heaven. Loves it and enjoys getting ready to go off each morning. Oh, happy day! I was so afraid she might not have been so eager.

Mary Ellen was launched, a milestone had been reached, but somehow it didn't register with Joan. It symbolized success, but also it made her aware of the years of training still ahead. Joan had a few hours to herself every day now, but didn't experience a sense of freedom. She worried constantly that Mary Ellen would be unable to keep up with her classmates. And Joan had to prepare for Mary Ellen when she came home each day. The work couldn't stop. On the contrary, Joan pushed harder so Mary Ellen would retain what she learned in school.

It seemed to Joan that she could never escape the world of deafness. She awoke to it each morning and went to bed with it every night. Often Dick would listen to her daily trials and fears and talk to her gently when she cried in frustration, anger, and sorrow for herself and for Mary Ellen. There were times when she wished she could be done with deafness forever. Yet it was now a familiar world. If she were with parents of normal children, talking about her plight would soon bore them. But she wanted to talk about Mary Ellen's successes and failures and swap stories with parents who had similar problems. Deafness was like her profession. She understood it and spoke the vernacular. It had become her life. That was why the clinic waiting room was so important. Joan talked to Claire or any of the other mothers, and they all understood each other.

"You should join the Lehigh Valley parents group," one clinic mother told Joan as they sat in the waiting room one afternoon. "My husband and I find it very helpful. You're dealing with parents from all walks of life who have deaf children. They have lectures and discussions and it's really very supportive."

It sounded ideal to Joan as a place where she and Dick could find the kind of adult support they lacked elsewhere in the community. But there was one hitch. Joan had become an expert on deaf education and knew that very few parents enrolled their children in programs similar to the clinic's. Beebe's method was oral, but she classified it as unisensory, and it was only one of a few centers in the country using the same method. There were numerous so-called oral programs where deaf children were taught to speak, but they also were allowed to learn lipreading and other forms of communication. Beebe believed that unless a child was forced to use hearing, he or she would never fully develop it to achieve comprehensible speech and usable language.

Joan knew that many of the education programs for the deaf in the United States were classified as total communication, or TC. These were multisensory programs in which children were taught to communicate through a variety of mediums, sign language, lipreading, even speech, if that developed adequately. What Joan had heard and experienced with Mary Ellen was that advocates of multisensory education really didn't believe that deaf children could be taught to hear and speak, and therefore channeled their children into the manual modes of communication. Joan met therapists who had trained in TC before discovering the unisensory method. They had never been instructed that deaf children could be taught to hear.

"Auditory training in college consisted of banging on a drum behind a child's head and asking how many times he or she heard it," one therapist told Joan. When the unisensory method was explained, the therapist tried it out on her students.

"I turned all the kids around and said 'hello.' But there was no response. It took time to realize that none of the children had been taught to use a hearing aid. Many had dead hearing aid batteries and broken cords."

"We taught the visual-tactile system," said another who had taught in a residential school. "This is a way of teaching speech in which my students would try to match my mouth movements when I spoke. They tried to figure out the right position through feeling my throat, matching my tensions, my way of making vowels and my voice quality. It was very artificial because they weren't learning to use their hearing."

Joan learned also that teachers in the residential schools

were expected to be surrogate parents, and the real mothers and fathers were excluded from the educational process. During the summer when they went home, the students learned very little or even regressed. Frequently they needed to relearn simple words like pencil, eraser, or book.

Joan knew how Beebe and the other therapists at the clinic felt about the multisensory approach. They believed that communication skills, such as sign language, had their place only after a deaf child had demonstrated an inability or unwillingness to learn language and speech through the development of residual hearing. The difference in philosophies had grown quite sharp and controversial over the years, and Beebe had been caught in the conflict from time to time.

Through the centuries there has been disagreement among educators of the deaf over whether their students could be taught to hear. By the end of the nineteenth century, however, they realized that the development of speech and hearing—the oral philosophy—was possible. At an international conference on deafness held in Milan in 1880, delegates resolved that the use of sign language was restrictive and slowed the development of speech and hearing skills. From that day until the mid-twentieth century, the emphasis in most countries has been on the oral philosophy of teaching the deaf.

The history of American education of the deaf after the Civil War is largely the struggle for dominance between the oral and manual philosophies, and the conflict still rages today. One of the main protagonists in the conflict in the latter part of the nineteenth century was Edward M. Gallaudet, the first president of Gallaudet College in Washington, D.C.

Ironically, Gallaudet was an early advocate of articulation and speech as an integral part of the education of the deaf, even though his name today is associated with the manual philosophy. At one point, Gallaudet was critical that some educators of the deaf did not devote enough attention to oral skills.

In 1868 Gallaudet convened a conference of principals of schools for the deaf. Those in attendance agreed that more attention should be placed on developing speaking and hearing skills and that courses in articulation and speech should be part of any curriculum. To some, Edward Gallaudet is regarded as the father of oral education in the United States. But it would not be long before he became a champion of the manual philosophy in an effort to counter an all-out assertion by some educators that the only proper philosophy was oral. Thus was born the conflict between the oral and manual philosophies. They have been at odds in this country for one hundred years and threaten to remain in conflict for decades to come.

Nevertheless, the controversy didn't seem to affect the Valley parents group, where both oral and TC families gathered for support. The group met once a month, and Joan and Dick became regulars. Joan found the sessions particularly useful because parents discussed new teaching methods and techniques that she could easily incorporate in her instruction. As time wore on it became apparent that most of the parents' children enrolled in TC programs were not advancing as quickly as Mary Ellen. Many had little or no vocabulary and could barely speak. Those who could were much more difficult to understand than Mary Ellen. Joan and Dick were reluctant to be spokesmen for the Beebe method. For one, they learned that some of the parents had different priorities than the total dedication of their lives and resources to overcoming their child's deafness. A new car or television set seemed more important to some. Others in the group couldn't afford the cost of Beebe's therapy. It was shattering to realize how few resources were available for something as basic as language training. It made Joan aware that she and Dick were fortunate. One woman was so impressed by Mary Ellen she visited the clinic and planned to enroll her child. But her husband died and everything changed. Another mother could not make the payments. She was heart-broken. Beebe carried the child as long as she could, free of charge.

Joan and Dick stuck with the parents group and became active participants at the weekly meetings. Joan even became public relations director. The big push for publicity always came in May, designated "Better Hearing Month," and the parents tried to place an article in the local newspaper relating to the problems of deafness. Joan sent an article to Polly Raynor, the women's editor of the *Allentown Morning Call*, and was surprised when Mrs. Raynor responded by setting up an appointment at the Hubers' for an interview. Mary Ellen had to be on her best behavior that day. A photographer took her picture with a talking doll, used to develop language, and another of Mary Ellen using the telephone. A third photo showed Mary Ellen with her classmates at the Beebe clinic.

When the article appeared, Joan read it carefully, leery that others in the group might see it as too strong an endorsement of the Beebe method. It was the truth, however, and she hoped that the parents of any deaf children in the area would either join the group or request additional information from the clinic.

The article concluded with Joan's dream "to erase the archaic image the public has of the deaf, and even erase the word 'deaf' itself. Because, there are virtually no totally deaf, there's always a remnant of residual hearing. We have discovered this first as parents of 'hard-of-hearing' children. Now we're eager to pass the word along."

"Mary Ellen is a curious child, her mother said. 'She explores everything about her and is self-reliant.'

"Her parents are convinced she's a bright child, too. She has a right to a normal life."

Not everyone in the *Morning Call* circulation area believed Mary Ellen had a right to a normal life. Shortly after the paper appeared on the Hubers' doorstep, the telephone began to ring and Joan was unprepared for the wave of resentment the article had generated.

"You are a very naive young woman," one caller asserted angrily. "I have a deaf son and I know that no amount of training will help him overcome his hearing loss. I think it's criminal that people like you hold out hope for the deaf."

"But there is hope," Joan replied, shocked at the vehemence of the attack. "How old is your son?" Joan asked. "If he started auditory training now . . ."

"Mrs. Huber!" the woman shouted. "I know my son is deaf and there is nothing I can do about it. I'm not so blind as to believe he can be taught to hear. Besides he has gotten an excellent education. Your statement that he will get the equivalent of an eighth-grade education is pure nonsense. He's gone to a school for the deaf and is very happy, thank you, and no thanks to people like you."

The line went dead. Joan gasped and laughed at the same time. She barely had time to pull herself together when the phone rang again. Throughout the morning she received a barrage of calls from mothers with deaf sons and daughters, all resentful that Joan could be so bold as to suggest that deaf children could be taught to hear and speak. Most callers had sent their children to residential schools for the deaf and took exception to the statement in the article that their children would graduate years behind their hearing contemporaries.

"I keep telling them the statistics are government figures, not my own," Joan told Grandmother Kennedy when she arrived for coffee at midmorning. "I don't understand how people can be so hostile about the truth. I was saying only that there is a better way to teach the deaf."

"They're hostile because it is the truth," Grandmother said. "It's probably too late for that better way or they can't afford it. The truth isn't easy to accept. They see you teaching Mary Ellen, giving her a normal life, and they don't want to hear about it."

The phone rang again, and Joan stood to answer it.

"Don't, Joanie. Let's get out of the house and wait for this to blow over," Grandmother said.

Joan was troubled as she and Grandmother Kennedy drove into Allentown. "I would think people would welcome new ideas and new methods," she said.

Grandmother Kennedy smiled. "Oh, Joanie, sometimes I believe you were born yesterday."

Joan spoke up as though she hadn't heard her mother. "I just sent a long letter to Nanette Fabray telling her all about the Beebe method. I guess I just assume that no one has heard of Beebe. I take it for granted that when they understand the unisensory approach they will take to it immediately."

It would be some months before Nanette Fabray, the actress who throughout the 1950s and 1960s publicized her struggle with her own hearing loss, responded to Joan. Joan was learning that there were many out there who didn't believe the Beebe method was the right approach.

Miss Fabray was very sympathetic to Joan's efforts to

teach Mary Ellen, but challenged Joan's assertion that sign language and finger spelling were a thing of the past. They are "very much alive," she said, a requirement for higher education of the deaf. In fact, she said, the strict oral philosophy was antiquated and warned that such an education would tend to retard Mary Ellen's mental development. It was obvious, too, that Miss Fabray's expectations for a deaf child did not go beyond institutions for the deaf. She told Joan that unless Mary Ellen learned manual methods of communication, she would be unsuitable for Gallaudet College and the Rochester Institute. She then added that the best advice she could give Joan on educating and rearing Mary Ellen was to allow Mary Ellen to associate with the deaf.

21

CHRISTMAS WAS COMING, and Mary Ellen was doing exceptionally well in nursery school. She was socially aggressive and not at all shy around her classmates. Her speech was showing improvement, and frequently she volunteered while other classmates were reticent.

"I really have no complaints about Mary Ellen," the teacher told Joan at an evaluation interview. "She's doing superbly and I wouldn't worry about her ability to survive in a public school environment. She thrives on it."

It was what Joan needed to hear. Mary Ellen showed great interest in her schoolwork and was progressing faster than Joan ever thought possible. Joan remembered Claire Davis's satisfaction when David started learning in class. Joan noticed it, too. She and the family were no longer the sole source of information in Mary Ellen's life. At the Huber family's annual Christmas gathering, Mary Ellen showed off her language ability and Joan no longer felt reluctant to discuss her deafness. Most of the family had become used to Mary

Ellen by this time and were often taken by her devilish charm.

Christmas was the usual madhouse. Mary Ellen did her part when she took a pair of Christmas scissors and cut off her eye lashes. In January Joan and Mary Ellen made the annual trip to Harrisburg for an audiogram and "knocked 'em dead," Joan recorded in her diary. The audiologists were astounded that a child with such a profound loss could hear so well. Beebe's theory was clearly working. The Hubers also received state aid for a second hearing aid. Mary Ellen still used only one aid with a Y-cord that connected to a mold in each ear. She would now have a separate aid for each ear, something Beebe had recommended for some time.

"There's no question that with two aids Mary Ellen will be able to hear much better," Beebe told Joan. "She'll pick up more sound and her incidental hearing will improve. That's when she'll detect conversation all around her."

Two aids made a difference. "Mary Ellen's teacher noticed a big change," Joan wrote. "She says she could see immediately that Mary Ellen was listening better." Mary Ellen was still doing well in class, "not at the head of the class," Joan noted, "but by no means is she bringing up the rear."

The winter continued and Joan was wearing down. Mary Ellen's resistance to the clinic stiffened as Beebe's demands grew. The trips to Easton were never dull, and Mary Ellen seemed to wreak havoc in borrowed cars. Joan drove her to Beebe's one afternoon in Grandmother Kennedy's car and was prepared to return it when she noticed the backseat area plastered with Grandmother's Green Stamps. Mary Ellen had struck back. Beebe was tightening the screws and sometimes walked out of the therapy room while Mary Ellen sulked and pouted. When Mary Ellen recanted, Beebe returned and the work resumed. Beebe stood behind her and issued commands. It was some of the toughest training Mary Ellen had experienced, but she had to learn to hear sound from all directions. She identified sounds and directives from behind, from the right and left. They studied books, cards, and pictures, over and over and over. The room was tiny and for an hour there was no respite. Beebe loomed above Mary Ellen. When it was over, Mary Ellen was ready to take her frustrations out on Joan. March arrived like a lion in the Huber house.

March 1. Kids sick—ugh! "Wizard of Oz" on TV last night. Mary Ellen understood the story. She knew that Dorothy wanted to go home, the scarecrow wanted to think, the tinman wanted a heart, and the lion wanted the courage so he wouldn't be afraid. The wicked witch melted.

March 2. Mary Ellen said a new word, "rash." You can guess why, she was covered with one. Last night we pumped up balloons and Mary Ellen learned the word "explode," and mom had a headache.

March 3. Mary Ellen seems to be picking up more and more from TV. Last night she called out "Gilligan save me." Then told me Gilligan exploded. She also said at the supper table, "Michael, don't be funny at the table"!!

March 6. Last day of confinement for my invalids. I have my application in for a rest home . . . was told I'm too young. I think they ought to take a look at me after this week. I make Ma Kettle look good. All the kids are terrifically bored. Grandfather Kennedy came over and punched out paper dolls with Mary Ellen. She was so happy to have someone else to play with that when he said he had to leave to go to work she said, "No, Grandfather, the steel is closed." Foxy. Mary Ellen now knows Sunday, Monday, Tuesday, Wednesday. That's four down, three to go.

March 15. Mary Ellen used the word "both," as meaning two. We saw the St. Patrick's Day parade and learned of shamrocks. It seems now all we have to do is tell her a word and she grasps the meaning. It doesn't seem to be the drilling and learning it used to be.

Joan doubled her efforts to train Mary Ellen's right ear, the one doctors said was dead. When Mary Ellen came home from nursery school each day Joan alternated by removing the ear mold from one ear each day. One day Mary Ellen was expected to listen using her left ear, the next day the right.

"Listen, Mary Ellen, listen," Joan said while working to improve the hearing in the right ear. "I want you to repeat after me. Listen, *da, da, da, da, da.*"

There was no response.

"Listen," Joan said in a loud voice. *"Da, da, da, da, da."* Mary Ellen sat next to her at the kitchen table. She seemed absorbed in something else.

"I want you to listen, Mary Ellen," Joan said firmly. *"Da, da, da, da."* She took Mary Ellen's hand and held it tight to gain her attention. "I won't let you do another thing until you repeat after me. Repeat, *da, da, da, da.*"

Mary Ellen looked up at Joan. She shifted in her chair but still did not repeat after her mother.

"Da, da, da," Joan repeated.

Mary Ellen got up from her chair and pushed it farther from Joan. Joan pulled it back.

"You will stay seated in your chair right next to me until you learn to repeat after me," Joan said. *"Da, da, da, da, da."*

Mary Ellen fidgeted and still did not respond to her mother's demand. Joan persisted. "Mary Ellen, you will not leave this table until you have repeated after me, *da, da, da, da.* You may not leave this table until you have repeated after me. *Da, da, da, da. . . ."*

Dick could sense the exhaustion and frustration when he stepped through the doorway that evening. The children were watching TV when he came into the kitchen. "I made her sit at that table for an hour and a half this afternoon until she repeated one simple syllable for me," Joan said.

"You're working with the right ear?"

"Yes. At this rate she'll be in her twenties before she can use it. Sometimes I wonder if I'll ever make it to see her through," Joan said. "It seems so endless, so futile. It takes weeks just to accomplish one simple goal. I just get so afraid that I won't make it. Sometimes I want to hang it all up."

But Joan carried on. If nothing else, she had to show the doctors. She'd become skeptical of physicians since Mary Ellen was born, although she still respected Dr. Rank. Joan had taken Mary Ellen to Dr. Rank for a checkup not long before when a medical student was assisting him for a few weeks.

"Joan, I want you to tell this young man all about Mary Ellen. Don't be kind to me or anyone else in our profession. Lay it on the line about how no one would listen," Dr. Rank said.

"Do you really want me to go into it all, Dr. Rank? You know I could be here all night." Joan laughed.

"Fine, be here all night. I want this future doctor to hear of a situation where the medical profession wasn't listening to the mother and the mother knew best all along. And listening is one of the most important things we can do." Joan's story didn't take all night. But after a half hour she saw the medical student had lost interest. Mary Ellen sat on the examining table flirting with the student, occasionally speaking to reinforce Joan's story.

At home the work continued on her right ear. *Da, da, da. Ca, ca, ca. Ma, ma, ma. Na, na, na.* Sounds, words, syllables were repeated over and over and over. It was exhausting, but it seemed to be working.

April 20. A really amazing thing happened today. Mary Ellen seems to be hearing from her right ear now and it doesn't appear to be guesswork. Hooray! Yippee and Hooray!

Summer was upon Joan before she had an opportunity to recover from the winter. The good news was that Mary Ellen had done well in nursery school and was enrolled in kindergarten for the following year. The weekly trips to the clinic continued until August, and Beebe expected Mary Ellen to learn a list of three hundred words during the summer. Joan was determined Mary Ellen would master them, but Mary Ellen was just as determined not to. Joan wrote the words in a notebook and awarded stars each time Mary Ellen used one correctly, and more stars when she used a word in a new context. The notebook followed them to the shore for a week at Long Beach Island, and on camping trips to the mountains.

Mary Ellen was happiest in August. The clinic closed, and she was free from the weekly trips to Easton. Almost daily she went to the swimming club, where she was at home in the water. Joan encouraged this independence but told the lifeguards that Mary Ellen would be unable to hear their warnings. At the beginning of the summer, a neighbor's two nieces came to visit for several weeks. The girls were the same ages as Mary Ellen and Kathy, and with Julie, the five played for hours on Troxell Street. The neighbor, Ruth, planned a trip into the Poconos and asked Kathy and Julie to accompany them.

"Doesn't Ruth like me?" Mary Ellen asked Joan.

Joan was angered but wouldn't reveal her feelings to Mary Ellen. Joan knew Ruth had avoided Mary Ellen because she would feel uncomfortable with a deaf child.

"No," Joan said. "Ruth likes you. It's just that if you went along there would be too many in the car. So they could only choose two. Ruth loves you very much."

Joan watched as Mary Ellen went into the basement and returned with an old guitar almost as big as herself. She carried the instrument onto the front porch and sat down and began strumming the strings as Ruth and the four girls prepared to leave. The strumming got louder as the departure time neared, and Joan cried at Mary Ellen's pathetic efforts to be noticed and accepted.

The new school year covered the summer's wounds.

September 15. Mary Ellen is now enrolled in Midway Manor Kindergarten. She takes to it like a duck to water. The school therapists feel we can be confident that Mary Ellen will hold her own and not to expect any big problems until the third grade, because she has enough language now to get her that far without too many complications.

October 15. Mary Ellen's teacher says Mary Ellen is a real doll—no problems—grasps things quickly. But she does say Mary Ellen has trouble answering abstract questions such as what do you think of the weather today. So what else is new?

There was progress on all fronts, and Joan prayed it would continue as nicely through the year. But during Mary Ellen's nightly bath, Joan noticed two lumps just at Mary Ellen's neck line, like the halves of a hard-boiled egg. Mary Ellen was so thin and reedlike that Joan wondered how they had gone undetected. Mary Ellen threw her head back while laughing and Joan saw the lumps protruding. Joan couldn't delay this time. She knew she had to act quickly. It wasn't just Mary Ellen's hearing that was at stake. It could be her life.

22

CHRISTMAS WAS A DELIGHT for Mary Ellen. She was bubbling with Christmas spirit and singing songs learned in kindergarten. Her favorites were "Jingle Bells" and "Santa Claus is Coming," and she constantly warned Kathy and Mike, "You better watch it."

But Christmas was less than joyous for Joan and Dick. An endocrinologist was hopeful, but would not rule out the possibility of malignancy and scheduled a thyroid scan for Mary Ellen in early January. Joan's fears increased because Aunt Marge was gravely ill, wasting away with a lung disease. The prognosis was poor. Grandmother Kennedy was constantly at her bedside trying to bring her cheer. There was a natural pall over the annual Huber Christmas party.

Mary Ellen's thyroid scan would not be easy. The doctors at the Allentown Hospital expected her to remain perfectly still, to not move a muscle while the massive head of the scan moved back and forth over her body. How do you keep a jitterbug quiet for more than a minute, Joan wondered.

"Mary Ellen, you must stay perfectly calm when the doc-

179

tor tells you. You can't move at all, otherwise we'll have to do the whole thing over again. When it's all done we'll go out and have a big treat."

Mary Ellen was subdued and for nearly an hour she lay still on the table in the strange room, sandbagged into place while the scan hovered above her. Joan held her hand tight, talking to her quietly, reassuring and amusing her. When it was over, Joan was proud. Mary Ellen could have screamed in terror. Joan had a growing admiration for her daughter, so controlled in adversity.

"Come on," Joan said to Mary Ellen after the procedure. "Let's go out to the gift shop and I'll buy you a big present."

It *was* a big present, too, $20 that Joan could hardly afford for a large, fluffy, stuffed cat.

The report was negative and Joan wept in relief, but the year was turning grim. By late spring Aunt Marge was slipping away and Grandmother Kennedy spent every day with her dying sister. Nothing could be done. By summer, when Mary Ellen finished kindergarten and was enrolled in first grade at Notre Dame in Allentown for the following year, Aunt Marge was in a Philadelphia hospital. She died in the fall.

The new school year would bring hope, Joan was sure. But it also brought renewed anxiety. Joan had always feared the first grade. This was the year that would put Mary Ellen to the test. The work was more demanding, and Joan was concerned that Mary Ellen couldn't keep up.

"She'll do just fine, Joan," Grandmother Kennedy said. "She's done so well these last two years I don't know why you're so worried. I think she's probably better prepared than any other children going into the first grade."

"Oh, you know, Mom, it's a mother's lot to worry. I'm always afraid that these years with Beebe have been a dream and it will come to a crashing end and all that those other people said will come true. We'll have to send her to special schools and she never will be able to talk normally."

"She's doing pretty well right now," Grandmother Kennedy said. She knew Joan needed a break from child rearing. "Send her over some time and she can do her homework at my house. I'll bring her back for supper."

"She'd love that," Joan said. Mike and Kathy occasionally went to Grandmother's house on their way home from school. It was special when the bus dropped them at Grandmother's. Once the homework was finished, Grandmother Kennedy made them treats or took them shopping. Now it was Mary Ellen's turn.

"I want to warn you, Mom," Joan said. "She is to do her homework. If she doesn't you must send her home immediately. No nonsense."

Mary Ellen was proud when the bus stopped at Grandmother's on the way home from school. Grandmother was waiting, prepared. She had seen Joan struggle with Mary Ellen for years and knew how difficult she could be to work with. Grandmother sat Mary Ellen down at the kitchen table and opened her books.

"Now, Mary Ellen, what is your homework assignment today?"

Mary Ellen chattered, but not about the schoolwork.

"Mary Ellen, we're here to do your homework. Let's not misbehave. Your mother told me that if you don't do it, I'm to send you right home."

Mary Ellen picked up a book and pretended to read, but was soon talking again. She rose from her chair. Grandmother had seen this performance before at Joan's. Mary Ellen would get out of her chair and refuse to get back in it.

"Mary Ellen, I want you in your chair right now!" Grandmother warned.

"Wait, wait."

"Right now," Grandmother said firmly. Mary Ellen ignored her.

"Mary Ellen," Grandmother Kennedy said quietly. "I am sending you home. I'll call your mother this moment so that she knows to expect you."

Mary Ellen looked at her grandmother incredulously. "No, no. Don't send me home." She sat down.

"No, Mary Ellen. I told you what I expected and you ignored me. Now you know you must obey if you wish to come back again."

Mary Ellen rose indignantly from the chair and picked up her books. She turned her back on Grandmother Kennedy, refusing to speak until she reached the door. As Grandmother Kennedy opened the door Mary Ellen looked her in the eye.

"You, you . . . you giant lady," she sputtered, searching her limited vocabulary for the proper epithet. "You big fat chicken." She wheeled and walked from the house.

"She's on her way home," Grandmother said as she called Joan. "And I'm now a giant lady and a big fat chicken."

Joan laughed the kind of laugh she always had with her mother. They chatted as Mary Ellen walked home.

"I have an appointment with the doctor," Grandmother said later that week.

Joan was perplexed. Grandmother made others see a doctor, but never went herself.

"What is the matter?" Joan asked.

"Just some bleeding. It's nothing big. Now don't worry."

But Joan was frightened. After Grandmother Kennedy's appointment with Dr. Rank, Joan called him immediately.

"Your mother has had this problem for a long time, Joan. It's bleeding from the colon. She should have come to me a lot sooner."

"Is it serious?"

"Bleeding of this nature can be. Why didn't she do something about it?"

"What do you plan to do?"

"I'm admitting her to the hospital for tests. We won't know till they're completed. Hang in there, Joan."

Joan waited anxiously for word from Dr. Rank. Mary Ellen didn't make it easy. She had been so well behaved in nursery school and kindergarten, but in first grade she showed signs of open rebellion. Joan knew the reason. Mary Ellen was bored. The first grade lessons at Notre Dame were new to most of her classmates, but they were familiar to Mary Ellen. The sister taught the same material Mary Ellen had had the year before. In desperation she called Joan.

"Mrs. Huber, every time I ask them to recite the alphabet, Mary Ellen picks up her desk and turns away from me and the class. I'm a little perplexed about what I should do."

"Picks up her desk?" Joan asked, startled.

"Yes, she defies me," the sister said.

"She'll have to be punished," Joan said. "What do you do for punishment?"

"I stand her in the hall."

"Do it."

Joan received another call the next day.

"I told her that she was to stand in the hall and I expected her to be there when I came out."

"Did she stand there?" Joan asked.

"No, Mrs. Huber, she didn't. She ran away and got her brother Mike and told him I had been mean to her."

"Well, punish her again," Joan counseled. "It's important

that you control her. She can be very difficult." The sister was aware of Mary Ellen's stubbornness. Joan had met with her at the beginning of the year and mentioned all Mary Ellen's quirks, but Joan hadn't expected such defiance. That was behavior Mary Ellen usually saved for home.

Grandmother Kennedy's tests had been completed, and Joan called Dr. Rank for the diagnosis.

"I'm sorry, Joan," Dr. Rank said quietly. "We found a malignancy in your mother's colon. There's no alternative but to operate."

Joan grieved.

"When will you operate?"

"Tomorrow or the next day. She's got the best specialists in Allentown and she'll be in good hands."

"What are her chances?" Joan asked.

Dr. Rank paused. "Joan, whenever there's cancer in the colon, it's a serious matter. But she's a tough woman. I think we'll bring her through. Let's pray for your mom and maybe our prayers will be answered."

Joan kept a vigil all next day at the hospital. She was there early and remained until Grandmother came back from the operating room in mid-afternoon. The surgeon was hopeful but his face was grim as he spoke quietly to Joan in the hallway outside Grandmother's room, still clothed in green operating room garb and cap.

The loss of Grandmother Kennedy would be unbearable and Joan tried not to dwell on it. There was much to keep her busy. Mary Ellen was progressing beautifully, but the work became more difficult as the expectation level rose. She was doing well in first grade, far better than Joan would have expected a few years before when her language and hearing ability were nil. But Joan still worried that Mary Ellen was bored in class. Beebe also demanded more with

184

each session, and although she never scolded Joan the way she did some parents, she always let Joan know when Mary Ellen was not performing well.

"Her speech is getting sloppy again," Beebe said. "Keep working on those *S*'s and *T*'s."

Joan was well aware of Mary Ellen's deficiencies, but there were times when the Huber family loved Mary Ellen's brand of the English language. Whenever she lost at a game, she stalked off in disgust. "I quick, I quick," she said, and the Hubers had a new word. "I quick, I quick," they would say whenever they wanted to drop out of a game or family function.

As she grew older, Mary Ellen was expected to help clear the table after supper. The children took turns clearing, scraping, and drying, and scraping was Mary Ellen's favorite task.

"I grape, I grape," she cried and again a new word was born. Chicken was schicken and squirrels were quirrels.

Amusing as her language was, it meant more hard work was ahead, and while Joan and Beebe bore down, Mary Ellen became more distant. The trips to the clinic were sometimes nightmarish. As a treat Joan gave Mary Ellen a pack of gum and the car was scented with peppermint to and from Easton. Joan assumed Mary Ellen was devouring her pack in several gulps and that accounted for the pervasive peppermint smell. Back home, however, Joan noticed stringlike strands hanging from the car's ceiling. Mary Ellen had chewed gum in massive wads, then strung it like clotheslines across the top of the car. As the interior warmed, the gum drooped in big arcs.

Increasingly Mary Ellen spent time alone in the therapy room as Beebe walked out and left her to her sulking moods. Joan listened to one session.

"Mary Ellen, I want you to concentrate," Beebe admonished. "You are not paying attention and I don't understand what you are saying."

Mary Ellen mumbled to Beebe.

"I didn't hear you," Beebe said.

Mary Ellen mumbled again.

"Speak up, I still can't hear you."

Mary Ellen said something almost inaudibly. Beebe rose from her chair and walked out.

"She told me I was the one who needed hearing aids." Beebe laughed.

Helping the new mothers was one way Joan forgot about Grandmother Kennedy's illness. By now she had developed a sophisticated method of teaching Mary Ellen, and her knowledge was useful in indoctrinating the newcomers. Generally Joan instructed them in an unused therapy room with old shoe boxes filled with everything Mary Ellen had collected and carried to her mother for identification. Across the table the young mothers sat nervously and expectantly, studying each item as Joan took it from the box and placed it on the table; feathers, acorns, pine cones, socks, string, books, and toys. It gave Joan satisfaction to work with new mothers who had just enrolled their children in the clinic. They were lost and afraid, hestitant and shy, as she herself had once been. Yet they were eager to teach their children and determined to succeed. They had to be. Like Joan, most had been counseled that there was no hope, yet they never gave up believing that there was some place where their children could be taught language.

Now Joan was the veteran, the pro teaching the rookies how it was done. And she was good, launching into her lecture that lasted more than an hour, spewing out information, insights, lessons, problems. She always had been a good talker, and no mother of a deaf child found her boring. Beebe asked every "old" mother to devote some time each month to teaching, and those who lived nearby gave as much time as they could.

"I've taught my daughter a million things with this junk," Joan said as she spread the contents on the tabletop. She laughed, knowing that at home she had shoe boxes stashed throughout the house and they were dubbed "crap boxes." The new mothers smiled at the worn and battered items. Joan picked up a Richard Scarry book that depicted a rainbow among the hundreds of drawings of animals, machines, utensils, and landscapes.

"This book is so full of things and you can expand on so many subjects. You know how vague a rainbow is. How do you tell a small child what it is? Well, here it is, and if it hadn't been for this book I don't know how I would have taught that to my daughter."

There was another small book that described all the sounds made by animals and machines. "One of Mary Ellen's teachers gave her a homework assignment to write a composition about Halloween. The children had to describe frightening sounds," Joan said. "How could she do that? I'd taught Mary Ellen words like cup, saucer, spoon. But how do you teach 'growl' or 'hoot'?"

Joan saw that she often got ahead of the young mothers across the table. She would pause. "Don't let all this stuff scare you. I've got to condense years of work into one hour and I have a tendency to overwhelm because I talk a lot and I am enthusiastic about the Beebe method. I should really say that I'm positively opinionated about this whole thing. You can't do it all at once, but it will all come together, in time."

"I found it to be very helpful to keep all the things Mary

Ellen would bring to me," Joan continued. "They are good teaching tools. Whenever your child approaches you, that's the best time to teach. The hardest time is when you have to drag them and sit them down. Take advantage of the times your child comes to you."

Joan pulled out an old athletic sock. "I used the sock because you can't look inside and cheat." Joan then placed three objects on the table, a miniature doll, a dollhouse cup, and a small block. "These were objects I knew Mary Ellen had mastered. It's important to use things the child knows in this game. You don't want to frustrate her—make it fun. You have to stay attractive to the child. You are the most important feature in a child's life. The child can get sick of Beebe but not of you.

"The beauty of the sock is not that children will identify the object inside, but will learn abstract concepts. They feel the sock. What do you *feel*?

"You ask them, 'Do you *remember* what's in the sock?' How do you teach remember? Only through repetition. You can't hammer at children and say 'remember, remember.' They'll be bored to death. You're playing with them and they pick up the idea from the demonstration. 'Did you *remember* what was in the sock? Did you *forget*?' How do you teach forget?" Joan would ask the mothers. "The sock is an excellent way.

"Let's say you put a toy cup in the sock and ask the child what is inside. The child says the cup and you say 'You are *right*.' You can make the distinction between right and wrong.

"Another lesson I devised was with flash cards showing various objects that were similar but with subtle differences. I'd ask Mary Ellen what was the *difference* between the objects. She loved playing that game."

Joan rooted through some of the objects on the table. "Don't be afraid to ham it up. The kids love that. You have to pretend a lot. Let them be the teacher and you pretend to make mistakes, and when they get things right you clap and cheer and carry on. It helps them learn. But most important, they don't get the feeling they are in a formal lesson. If it's fun they can do it for a long time. If it's drudgery, they'll never acquire language."

Joan also suggested that the family buy a dictionary of idioms and start teaching them as quickly as possible. "You run into snags with idioms. Deaf kids just don't understand them the way normal hearing children do. They take them literally." Joan remembered the story Claire had told about David. After one session with Beebe, David was perplexed. Later Claire learned that Beebe had used the term "pulling your leg." David had waited, but Beebe had not reached down and tugged.

Joan urged her new mothers to ask any questions that came to mind. "Nothing is too silly to ask," she said. "Take it one day at a time. Incorporate all these lessons into the day and have others help you whenever possible. My family helps all the time and so does my mother. She's great."

Joan's thoughts were never far from her mother and the days she was healthy. Joan smiled when she remembered Grandmother Kennedy cleaning the children all the time. They were always into something sticky or gooey, always looked like street urchins. Joan didn't have the time or the inclination to keep them clean. Grandmother did. She had them well scrubbed and behaving properly. Joan prayed the operation would bring good news. Even if it didn't, though, Grandmother Kennedy would be around at least five years. That was Joan's one great consolation.

23

GRANDMOTHER KENNEDY WAS SUBDUED at Christmas when the Huber clan had their traditional gathering. Throughout the winter her condition failed to improve and by St. Patrick's Day she was back in the hospital. It meant additional responsibilities for Joan. She spent hours with her mother each day, then rushed home to take care of the kids and struggle with Mary Ellen's lessons. The dizziness returned, as did the heart flipflops. They were annoying, but Joan had long since learned to live with them. She knew their cause. She was grieving over her mother's illness, praying Grandmother Kennedy would get well. Dr. Rank hadn't said anything discouraging, so there was hope.

Mother's Day that year was a major event for the Hubers. Grandmother Kennedy had just been released from the hospital, exhausted, but up and around. The following Sunday the entire family went to mass. It was Kathy's first communion, and Grandmother felt strong enough to come along. Kathy's formal acceptance into the Catholic Church was an event Grandmother would never miss.

A special pew was set aside for the Huber family. The congregation didn't notice. When it was time for the Offertory, the priest smiled and announced:

"If the ushers have selected someone in the congregation to bring up the offering, I would ask them to please let the Huber family bring up the gifts this Sunday. Mr. Huber will receive his first communion today. It's taken Mr. Huber ten years to make up his mind and we don't want anything to get in his way."

As weak as she was, Grandmother was thrilled. Dick finally had decided to become a Catholic. It was only natural. Every Sunday for a decade he had accompanied his children to church and attended all church functions. He also had stood over Mike, Kathy, and Mary Ellen as they completed their religious studies each week. But he had kept his plans to join completely to himself, going for instruction when Joan was with Grandmother Kennedy in the hospital. He didn't require a lengthy instruction period. He'd been exposed to Catholicism so long it almost came naturally. Dick's first communion was the last mass Grandmother was able to attend.

But the joy of that Sunday was soon lost. Grandmother's condition worsened. On Mother's Day she was readmitted to the hospital. Joan was heartbroken. No one had told her, but she sensed it. They were nearing the end.

Her mother was not the same woman as before. She was wasted and tired and for the first time she and Joan didn't open their souls to each other. Joan was by her side most of the day, leaving toward evening when the kids needed attention. Uncle Eddie, Joan's brother, and Grandfather Kennedy kept the vigil with Joan, and took over when she wasn't there. The reality of Grandmother's condition devastated Joan, but she couldn't bring herself to believe that her mother was dying.

"Mom looks just terrible!" Joan told Dr. Rank the day after Grandmother Kennedy went back in the hospital. "It's her coloring that scares me. Isn't there anything you can do for her? She's the shade of an oyster." Joan was near tears.

Dr. Rank put his hand on Joan's shoulder.

"I've always been honest with you, Joan. I haven't said anything about your mother because you haven't asked and I didn't feel it necessary to make matters worse by telling you." He paused. "Joan, your mother is dying. There's nothing that can be done. That's why her coloring is so poor. She hasn't got much time."

Dr. Rank's words were distant and unreal. Yet they weren't unwelcome. Now all the uncertainty was over.

"I knew she'd never be the same," Joan said quietly. "But I thought we'd at least have her a couple more years."

"I was hoping for that too," Dr. Rank said. "The thing to do now is to make her as comfortable as possible. That's going to be difficult."

As the disease spread, Grandmother Kennedy's pain intensified and Joan watched helplessly. The doctors prescribed pills that worked briefly. Grandmother bore up under it stoically and refused to bother Joan with her torment.

"It's the first time Mom and I haven't talked turkey," Joan said to Dick as they sat quietly in the living room after the kids had gone to bed. Eddie was with Grandmother Kennedy and Joan would return early in the morning after the children had gone to school. "I think she's sparing me. I think she knows." Joan's voice trailed off.

Joan spoke quietly in tired, measured tones. There also were moments of silence when Joan and Dick contemplated their world without Grandmother Kennedy. It would be strange without her. Joan fought off a sense of panic. How would she ever manage without Grandmother Kennedy?

Who would care for the children as well? Even Joan's religion did not sustain her. She had grown up fearing God as much as loving Him, and as a child the priests had frightened her because they presented a harsh God. God could be vindictive and cruel, the way he was now in taking her mother.

The days dragged on. Grandmother Kennedy's condition worsened; the pain was now almost constant. She lay helpless as Joan and Eddie watched her slowly slipping away.

"There's only one thing to do," a doctor said to the family. "We've got to operate to relieve the pain. The malignancy has invaded the kidneys and we've got to clear them."

"The sooner the better," was Grandmother's reply. Joan held her hand tightly as she was rolled out to the operating room, and then waited alone. Grandmother returned several hours later, heavily sedated. When finally she awoke, Joan was hurt by the resignation in her eyes, dim and sad. Joan felt the gulf, the separation, as though her mother already had started her journey.

Joan and Eddie continued their watch. It was morning, and Joan had just arrived at the hospital, dizzy from apprehension and sadness. She talked quietly to her mother. Suddenly a queer expression came over Grandmother Kennedy's face. A shrill beeping filled the room, and Joan heard hurried footsteps in the hall. She saw a blur of white as several nurses rushed into the room. The hallway echoed with voices: "Code Blue, Code Blue."

Joan watched wide-eyed, disbelieving, as nurses and interns stripped off Grandmother Kennedy's gown, exposing her frail body. There were short commands and more footsteps pounding in the hallway as people converged on the room. Joan slipped into the hall. Her mother was dying.

"You may come back in the room now, Mrs. Huber."

Joan looked warily at the nurse who approached her from Grandmother Kennedy's room.

"We pulled her through," the nurse said.

Joan entered and saw her mother. Grandmother Kennedy's face was worn and old. Joan hardly recognized her; there was little resemblance to her mother when she was a young woman, the way Joan would always remember her, slight and dark. Age and disease had transformed her. She breathed quietly and regularly, but was unconscious. Joan sat stonelike the rest of the day. Grandmother Kennedy's condition remained unchanged.

A doctor appeared late in the day.

"How's your mother?"

"The same," Joan said softly.

"Why did you do that to her?" he asked.

"Do what?" Joan asked.

"I know you must love your mother, but why?"

"I'm afraid I'm not following you," Joan said.

"The operation. You should never have put her through that. You're just prolonging her agony."

Joan was startled by the man's candor, angered by his misdirected advice and audacity.

"I was advised to have the operation to help my mother. And that advice came from several doctors," Joan said.

"I think it would have been better never to have gone through with it," the doctor said.

Joan remained by her mother's side. Grandmother came out of her coma briefly, then lapsed back into unconsciousness.

Eddie joined the vigil. "Why don't you go home?" he said. "It's past eight and the kids will need you in the morning." It had been two days since Grandmother fell into a coma.

"I'd rather not," Joan said looking over at her mother. "I want to be with her when she goes."

"Go home, Joan. We may be here a long time."

She drove through the darkened streets of Allentown, across the Lehigh River toward home. Dick was waiting with dinner. The kids were in bed. Joan's face told him the whole story.

"Any change?"

"None."

Joan slept fitfully through the night, waking frequently. She watched the phone and remembered her mother in younger days. Joan was too numb to weep. At five in the morning the phone rang.

It was Eddie's voice, and Joan was prepared by his quiet tone.

"Mom's gone."

Joan paused, absorbing the blow. It was less severe than she expected.

"I'm glad," she said. "She didn't deserve to suffer so badly."

24

MARY ELLEN BEGAN SECOND grade in the fall after Grandmother Kennedy's death. It was a hectic, sad time for Joan.
There was no one to pop in after she got the kids off to
school. The house seemed empty. Joan let Mary Ellen settle
in class for a week before she approached the teacher.

"Hello, Sister, I'm Joan Huber."

"Oh, yes," the sister said. She was a stocky woman approaching middle age and wore the traditional teaching garb
that included dark slacks. "You're Mary Ellen's mother."

Joan smiled. There was nothing ominous about this
woman. She had a pleasant face that calmed Joan's fears. She
always worried that Mary Ellen would wind up with a hu-
morless, intolerant teacher who refused to take the time to
work with a deaf child. "I always drop by after the first week
to acquaint teachers with Mary Ellen's condition." Joan
placed a manila envelope on the sister's desk as she sat
down. It contained Mary Ellen's "SOS" book, copies of her
audiogram, and teachers' instructions from the Beebe clinic.
Joan handed the SOS book to the teacher.

"I give this to all Mary Ellen's teachers. You write down any problems she is having and we can work on them at home. This way you won't have to call me and won't feel the need to approach me when you see me in the hall. I'm a volunteer mother at Notre Dame and you'll see me often."

The sister picked up the audiogram and studied it carefully. "I can see from this that Mary Ellen is profoundly deaf," she said. "You'd never know it from the way she manages in class."

These were words of encouragement for Joan. She crossed her fingers that Mary Ellen would continue to do well.

"You seem to know something about deafness," Joan said.

"Yes, I do," the sister said. "I spent a number of years teaching in a residential school for the deaf and I can assure you, Mary Ellen is way ahead of most of those poor children. It's remarkable. I never would have guessed that a deaf child could perform so well."

"We have her in a special program in Easton," Joan said as she described the Beebe method. She scrutinized this new teacher as she spoke. On the one hand she was happy that the sister had worked with deaf children. But Joan worried that she would not devote enough time to Mary Ellen. The sister had never worked with deaf children who had the ability to hear and speak and she might ignore Mary Ellen altogether.

The weeks passed, and Mary Ellen did well. Joan kept her promise not to approach teachers and the sister put few entries in the SOS book. There were problems with pronunciation, and Mary Ellen didn't understand certain words. It was at home where Mary Ellen had most of her troubles. Every day Joan awaited the return of the three children with trepidation. She required all three to sit down immediately and do their homework. Mike usually went to his room to study. Kathy and Mary Ellen sat at the kitchen table, where they squabbled with each other, and Joan struggled to get Mary Ellen to study.

"Here we go again on that old roller coaster ride," Joan said to herself as she saw the children coming up the driveway to the back door that opened into the kitchen. In the spring and summer, the neighbors became used to the clamor of voices from the Huber kitchen. Grandfather Kennedy occasionally read his newspaper outside on the terrace. But when the kids came home, he left for home and quiet.

"Mary Ellen, I want you to sit down and do your homework," Joan said.

Mary Ellen made moves toward the chair, pushed it to one side, stood behind it, then returned it to its original position at the table.

"Mary Ellen, I want you in your chair immediately!"

"In a minute."

"In your chair," Joan ordered.

Mary Ellen sat in the chair, her slender body bouncing as Joan pushed a second grade primer under her nose.

"I wanna go to the bathroom," Mary Ellen complained.

"You can do that later," Joan said.

"No, now!"

"No, Mary Ellen. You are going to do your homework, NOW."

"I need to go to the bathroom," Mary Ellen whined.

"OK, Mary Ellen, go. When you come back, you will do your homework by yourself. I'm not going to help you."

Mary Ellen suddenly stopped, the need to go to the bathroom forgotten. She looked helplessly at her mother.

"But you don't want to help me. I won't be able to do it right."

Joan was used to the guilt trip. But it was true. Unless Joan helped Mary Ellen, she frequently couldn't do her homework. She needed her mother's supervision. "Then get back in your chair," Joan ordered. Mary Ellen returned obediently. Joan opened the book and they began. Mary Ellen's concentration held for a few minutes as they reviewed a chapter, then Joan could feel it slip away as Mary Ellen became more restless. Mary Ellen got down from the chair.

"Mary Ellen!"

"Wait one minute."

"No, get back here immediately," Joan warned. Mary Ellen looked at her mother, and stalled.

"OK, Mary Ellen, that's it. You are going to do your homework by yourself. And tomorrow you'll have to explain to sister why you had so many mistakes."

"Because my mother doesn't help me," Mary Ellen wailed.

"I'm not going to help you," Joan said as she rose from the chair and walked toward the living room. Mary Ellen followed close behind.

"Please don't do that," Mary Ellen pleaded.

"No, not until you behave yourself and today it's too late."

"But I won't be able to do it," Mary Ellen said as she followed Joan up the stairs to the bathroom. Joan got there first and closed the door quickly. She locked it and stood in the bathroom trying to control her frustration and anger.

"Please come out and help me," Mary Ellen cried from the other side of the door. She knocked and then pounded on the door, begging her mother to come out.

"I locked myself in the bathroom to get away from her today," Joan told Dick that evening. "I can't believe the things I'm doing because of Mary Ellen. There I was, a woman of thirty-four, locked in the bathroom while my seven-year-old is banging on the door pleading with me to come out and help her with her homework. I felt like an idiot and a child."

Dick understood. Occasionally his mild manner would crack when he watched Joan work with Mary Ellen after dinner. Mary Ellen had a repertoire of tricks to thwart even the most patient, and Dick would raise his voice and demand that she behave. It was his deeper voice, if anything, that startled Mary Ellen. She would look up and see his normally placid face red with anger. Dick approached, warning that he would discipline her. Mary Ellen sat up straight, her body becoming rigid in the chair. She turned her head away from her father and quickly flicked off her hearing aids. Dick moved closer, and Mary Ellen closed her eyes. He came no farther.

Mary Ellen's behavior concerned Joan, and once or twice she broke her vow and approached the sister.

"How is she doing?" Joan asked. "Are you having any particular difficulties with her?"

"None, Mrs. Huber," the sister reported.

But almost daily Mary Ellen acted out her rebellion at home. And Joan and Dick tried to combat the behavior. But there were always distractions. Joan discovered another lump on Mary Ellen, this time in the breast area. Joan wasn't as alarmed, but Dick took it seriously. The Hubers had had their share of cancer. It was several days before Joan took Mary Ellen to the doctor, again with the complaint of a lump under the skin.

"Nothing really to worry about," Dr. Rank reported.

"What is it?" Joan asked.

"Oddly enough it happens in both boys and girls. It's a

gland that's showing signs of development. That's all. But I can understand your concern."

Joan picked up the phone and called Dick at the office "The doctor says it's nothing to worry about," Joan said.

Dick could feel the relief, then the welling emotion. He burst into tears.

25

DICK KNEW THE ANGER and frustration Mary Ellen could raise in both Joan and himself from the knock-down, drag-out struggle they went through to teach her language. Yet beneath it was empathy for his daughter, especially when he saw Mary Ellen in her Notre Dame outfit, a navy blue plaid jumper, white blouse, navy blue knee socks, saddle shoes, and the ever-present vest that carried her two hearing aids. She looked like a tiny body running around on toothpicks.

He recollected the saga of the saddle shoes. Mary Ellen had wanted them for months, but her feet were so slender it was difficult to find any that fit. She persisted and Joan agreed to buy a pair, but not without a hefty condition. Mary Ellen first had to master Beebe's three hundred words during the summer. It was another battle, but by the beginning of third grade Mary Ellen had her shoes. They were her pride, offsetting the vest she had to wear. Joan made her a new vest every school year, but Mary Ellen disliked wearing it and developed a slouch trying to hide the two aids that fit into pockets at breast level.

Joan and Dick watched in silence as Mary Ellen suffered because of deafness, knowing they could not intervene. Sometimes she was ridiculed for the way she talked, and Joan knew she was wounded more than Mike and Kathy had ever been. Yet Mary Ellen seldom complained. She would have to deal with the handicap her own way, and Joan knew that Mary Ellen's brand of stubbornness would pull her through. Mary Ellen would not be put down; she bullied her way into acceptance, fought, manipulated, even clowned to get her way. Joan knew Mary Ellen didn't follow all the conversation around her, yet she pretended to be right in the thick of things.

She also knew that for Mary Ellen, and all deaf children, a tremendous amount of communication is nonverbal. Any deaf child, no matter how adept at hearing, learns to read lips, cheeks, gestures, and body language. They become masters of nonverbal speech, listening and concentrating on lips, watching expressions and gestures to make up for what they miss through their hearing. Mary Ellen was unable to detect subtle and distant sounds that the hearing took for granted—the rustle of leaves, the soft rush of the breeze, or distant footsteps on the pavement. To the deaf like Mary Ellen and David hearing is a miraculous ability.

The instruction at the clinic continued unabated, tougher than before. Beebe and Mary Ellen reviewed Mary Ellen's weekly experience book in which Joan and Mary Ellen recorded the major events of the week. Daddy was sick in bed, Joan was stopped for speeding on Route 22, and the basement was flooded. Mary Ellen was expected to describe all the events.

They read books, named objects on flash cards, worked on pronunciation, sounds, and chewing. Beebe stood behind Mary Ellen issuing commands, and Mary Ellen carried them out. Mary Ellen squirmed, Beebe became more demanding, and Joan talked with Claire Davis in the waiting room.

David was in his catastrophe stage, consumed by earthquakes, volcanic eruptions, fire, and wrenching, screeching wrecks. Claire had gotten him a Big Brother to take him away from the family environment for several hours each week. And his favorite haunts were demolition derbies and auto junkyards. After a visit to a wrecking yard, David would run to his room and smash his toy cars.

He stole his sister's Barbie dolls and hurled them to the sidewalk below. They were "victims" jumping from a fire or blown from explosions or earthquakes. They sailed down to the pavement, and if they "crumped" just right, their heads popped off and rolled down the sidewalk while the bodies lay lifeless on the ground.

Claire later laughed at the antics of her son, who also was the bane of his older sister, Lisa. David had used Lisa's favorite dollhouse to simulate the force of an earthquake. Four beautifully decorated rooms were transformed into a disaster area as David vibrated the dollhouse into ruins. David had also developed a memory like Mary Ellen's. In second grade he was the best speller in the class, winning all the spelling bees. He had the same ability with numbers and served as the Davises' telephone directory.

"If we want to telephone the electric company, Bell Telephone, or the police, we just ask David," Claire said. "He knows all the numbers. People tell him their numbers and he'll remember them months later. We ask him and he'll say, 'Want the area code too?' He doesn't remember names, but he'll remember street addresses. I think it's an ability developed to compensate because of his deafness."

"How's he doing in school?" Joan asked.

"Beautifully," Claire said. "He's made remarkable progress.

Last year in first grade he was reading well and was able to understand most of what went on in class. But I'm so happy with his achievement tests. He's scored above average in five of six categories."

It hadn't always been that way. Claire explained how two years before David had tested at a level of the functionally retarded. It was a typical problem for the deaf. Deaf children whose language skills are less than adequate are sometimes given tests designed for hearing children. David was given such a test when he was five years old and the results were devastating.

"If Jim and I hadn't been there to overhear the testing we would have been very upset," Claire said. "It was bad enough having a psychologist tell us our son was sub-par. Beebe was her wonderful self throughout. She told us to ignore the results. David was given the same test a few years later and was identified as gifted."

David was an impressionable kid, manipulated because of his deafness. He had gone to a school in downtown Easton with less advantaged kids. They found David easy prey. In the big old classroom, some of the less disciplined boys dragged David into hiding places or took him into the bathroom where they capitalized on a quirk in the plumbing. If the toilets were flushed twice they all overflowed.

"But now that he's in the second grade he's doing much better," Claire said. "He's accepted, although it's still difficult for him. You know how kids are, they can be very cruel and occasionally he comes home hurt. I think it's tougher on the parents to see a hurt child than it is on the child."

She laughed. "His teacher tells a funny story about the first several days David was in class. She had no idea what to expect from a deaf child. Well, she thought one of the children was whistling whenever her back was turned and she

205

kept expecting to catch the culprit in the act. But no one was doing it. She finally realized the whistle came from David's hearing aids. The molds were loose."

Claire admitted that second grade was still tough. David had been unable to write a sentence at the beginning of the year and Claire and the teacher worked with him until he could. "He'd have the noun at the end and the verb at the beginning. It was so frustrating because I'd think he had learned the correct way to write, and he would backslide and show no understanding of sentence structure. But I think we've got it now."

Talking to Claire was helpful, but it also magnified the size of the task that was only half finished. Even then, Beebe recommended that her older students continue therapy just to refine their speaking and listening skills. Joan wondered if she would be able to keep Mary Ellen at the clinic that long.

26

JOAN EXPECTED THIRD GRADE to be another test of Mary Ellen's abilities. She would have to master multiplication and other work more sophisticated than that in the two previous years. The children would be dealing with concepts and abstractions. Still, Joan promised herself not to intervene after her initial meeting with the teacher. She dropped off her SOS book and went home to wait for disaster to strike. It never came.

Mary Ellen had her usual problems with listening, and her vocabulary remained limited compared to her classmates. But the notations in the SOS book were sparse. Joan began to wonder again if the teacher was effectively dealing with Mary Ellen. Then came a surprise. The teacher sent home a notation that, indeed, there was a problem. Mary Ellen had mastered her schoolwork so well that she could no longer take part in the math bingo game held each day. The teacher would ask the class questions and the students able to answer received a prize. Mary Ellen was walking away with every prize and annoying her classmates.

Mary Ellen's performance was a relief for Joan. She couldn't say catergorically that Mary Ellen had succeeded in overcoming deafness. There were still too many improvements to be made. But Mary Ellen was on the way, doing well in school, communicating with her friends and adults, and gaining acceptance among her classmates. She was far from being the typical deaf child unable to communicate with language and hearing. Dick got a taste of what these children were like when his job took him to a nearby school for the deaf. He thought it pathetic that children Mary Ellen's age could neither hear nor speak and that those who did speak were virtually incomprehensible. Most of the children used sign language and finger spelling, and their "speech" was wild gesticulations and occasional grunts. Classes were generally taught with sign language, and the academic pace was slow.

Joan wasn't the only clinic mother whose child was doing well in school. At their meetings in the clinic waiting room, they exchanged stories. Claire too had been worried. She'd introduced herself to David's teacher and been disturbed by her attitude. The teacher seemed nonchalant about David's deafness. Claire went home, afraid David would languish in the classroom. Hearing nothing from the teacher about his performance, she frequently dropped by to ask how David was doing. Finally the teacher looked at her and said quietly and pointly, "Mrs. Davis, when David learns to work independently, he will have accomplished something."

"I was no fool," Claire said to Joan. "She was telling me she wanted David to cut the apron strings. She told me that if David encountered a problem, she'd let me know."

There were no problems. Like Mary Ellen, David had difficulty hearing everything the teacher said, and his vocabulary was limited. But from his first report card it was obvious that he too was doing exceptionally well. His teacher said little to Claire, but she expected more of David than many of his classmates. She knew he was bright and capable and sensed that discipline and high expectations were the keys to his success. If he was daydreaming, she refused to hear the excuse that he couldn't hear. She took his desk and pulled it in front of the class.

"Since he's been in third grade, Jim and I aren't doing any more for David than any conscientious parent would do for his child," Claire said. "We're there to encourage and offer support, but he's the one who's got to have the determination to succeed. Now I can go out and get hit by a truck and know that David will graduate from high school."

It wasn't quite that easy for Joan, but she knew Mary Ellen had the determination to master the language. She had succeeded already, and not even the experts knew Mary Ellen was profoundly deaf. This was apparent on a trip to the hearing center in Philadelphia. It had been several years since Joan had Mary Ellen's hearing tested at the hospital, and Beebe suggested she take Mary Ellen back for her yearly audiogram and show the audiologists Mary Ellen's progress. In particular, Beebe suggested, they should see that Mary Ellen was using the ear they said was useless.

"I think they would be most interested to see how well Mary Ellen is doing. Maybe you can change their attitude about deafness and demonstrate that it is possible to develop hearing and speech."

Joan was game. She had great pride in Mary Ellen's accomplishments and what better way to show them off than to let the pros see how far she had come in four years. Joan set up an appointment and they drove down several weeks later. The center had changed little since Mary Ellen had been there as a small child. She went through the preliminary tests and was scheduled for the standard hearing examination in which she wore headphones and signaled the audiologist when she heard a tone. Joan was brimming with pride, but was deflated somewhat when a different audiologist approached them.

"Hello," he said. "This must be Mary Ellen."

He was a short, slender man, an Indian or Near Easterner.

"This is Mary Ellen," Joan said.

"Hi," Mary Ellen spoke up.

"What grade are you in?" the audiologist asked.

"Third grade! You look like my Uncle Eddie," Mary Ellen said.

"Why is that?" the doctor asked in his thickly accented voice.

"Cause you have a mustache just like my Uncle Eddie."

The man smiled. "You speak very, very well, Mary Ellen," he said. "Why don't we proceed with the test?" He picked up Mary Ellen's charts and tucked them under his arm.

"You must take off your hearing aids, young lady," he said. "But before you do, let me give you instructions. When you hear the tone in the headset, I want you to push this lever. That will indicate to me that you have heard the sound."

Mary Ellen dutifully removed the ear molds and sat down in the soundproof booth. She waited as the doctor worked at his console, turning a dial to create the various tones. He looked questioningly at Joan and continued to turn the dial. Only twice did Mary Ellen respond to the sounds. The audiologist stood up, took the file, and pulled out the audiograms. He studied them for a moment, then strode over to Joan.

"Mrs. Huber, your daughter is profoundly deaf!"

"Yes, I know," Joan replied.

"Somebody has been working very, very hard with Mary Ellen."

"Yes. I have and she goes to a wonderful clinic in Easton where they stress development of hearing."

The audiologist looked earnestly at Joan.

"Do you have other children beside Mary Ellen?"

"Yes, we have a boy two years older than Mary Ellen and a daughter who is eleven months older."

"Do you ever spend any time with them?" the audiologist asked.

"Of course," Joan replied with a short, perplexed laugh. "They are my children."

"But how can you not neglect them if you spend all this time with Mary Ellen?"

"I don't neglect them," Joan asserted. "I'm able to spend time with them and my husband spends a great deal of time with our son. Besides, they have grandparents and aunts and uncles and come from a close, supportive family."

"But they will suffer from all your attention to Mary Ellen and . . ."

"I really don't understand what you mean. They are not neglected."

The audiologist interupted. "You know Mary Ellen will grow up to be a very emotionally disturbed child."

"What!"

"Oh, Mrs. Huber, Mary Ellen may be doing fine right now, but when she gets older, she won't be able to keep up. Her training will do her serious harm. You must not do this to her."

Joan would hear no more. She grabbed Mary Ellen and left. "When will I ever find a doctor or audiologist who isn't living in the Middle Ages?" she said to Dick that evening.

"Where do these people get their ideas? They should know better. How could any reasonable man say such garbage?"

Wherever she turned now, she seemed assaulted by doubters. Once again she picked up her pen to strike back in a letter to a newspaper, this time thc *Allentown Evening Chronicle.*

Dear Editor,

Recently there were two articles published in your newspaper regarding the deaf.

The one article (March 18th) was on the sign language classes being taught at a local hospital. The other article (February 4th) was on a new clinic being opened to help in the diagnosis of the deaf and as a center of information for the deaf once the diagnosis was ascertained.

As a parent of a profoundly deaf child, I am deeply concerned about the issues these articles raised: Deafness is a grossly neglected handicap. While it can be a far less tragic handicap than mental retardation, blindness, or a crippling disease, without early diagnosis and proper treatment (speech therapy) deafness can be even more tragic than these. As parents of a deaf child our experience is identical to many parents in this area. Our child was diagnosed as profoundly deaf and we were given two alternatives: send her to a residential school for the deaf or keep her at home and provide her with private speech therapy. This private therapy, we were told, would be very expensive and couldn't guarantee results. However, if we chose a residential school the state would assume the financial burden. But there was more than finances to be considered. Keeping her at home, supported by private therapy, offered her at least a chance at speech and a normal life. At a residential school she would learn sign language and ultimately communicate and live with only the deaf—in a truly deaf world.

We decided to keep her at home and enrolled her in a program of speech and hearing therapy which uses the "auditory" approach. She was fitted with powerful hearing aids and through therapy gradually began to use her hearing and to develop speech. Now, six years after making our decision, we are confident that it was the right one and we want to alert the professionals who indifferently tried to guide us away from the best possible means of education of our deaf daughter, to the consequences that their indiscreet advice could have held for her.

Annually our child is given a hearing test with results that defy explanation. The audiologist will say, 'My those hearing aids are doing a terrific job,' ignoring the fact that there are countless children with the same hearing aids and the same hearing losses, but with no speech or language. They never question the difference because there are always twelve more people to be examined and there is never any spare time. Hearing aids are not like eyeglasses—the child must be trained how to use them. This is auditory training and this is what makes the difference. But it is costly. For us there is no price tag for what our child has achieved. But—how many more children would have had this privilege if it weren't so costly and if those people who counsel parents would take the time to really investigate the auditory approach to training the deaf.

There are areas all over the world using the auditory method successfully, and it has been in this area for the past thirty years. Yet it continues as private speech therapy with no state or federal support. The irony is that by keeping the child at home the parents save the state approximately $5,000. Yet, the private therapy at a cost of $800 per year must be entirely absorbed by the parents. This expense, together with the cost of hearing aids, batteries, evaluations, etc., is overwhelming for some families—impossible for many others. We feel if professional people would lend support and get behind the parents who chose auditory training, perhaps together we could get state recognition and offer all deaf children this opportunity and not just those able to afford it. These children deserve a chance at a normal life in a hearing and speaking world.

Respectfully,
Mrs. Richard Huber

Mary Ellen was certainly on her way to a normal life. She had no trouble adjusting in third grade. In fact, Joan worried that she was becoming too much of a social butterfly. She laughed to herself. "Who ever would have thought a few short years ago that Mary Ellen would be so socially accepted?" Her language was improving constantly and her hearing was nearly perfect. She knew how to lip-read but did not need it to get along. She used her lipreading ability to do magic tricks. Mary Ellen's teacher informed Joan that Mary Ellen had developed a new one. She would stand behind a glass door while her friends on the other side mouthed the words. The challenge was for Mary Ellen to guess whatever they said. She was rarely wrong.

27

DESPITE THE PROGRESS, the challenges continued. Grandmother Kennedy's death left a void that would be impossible to fill and Joan found herself turning to the church for support. She never had doubted its importance in her life, but there was always a reluctance to embrace her faith wholeheartedly. That smacked of fanaticism and she was embarrassed by those who wore religion on their sleeves. Above all, though, she had never felt totally comfortable with the Catholic Church. She still viewed its God as unloving, its precepts as too narrow.

It was some time after Grandmother Kennedy's death that Joan joined a Catholic retreat at a nearby convent. For an entire weekend she and a group of women talked about their passage through life, where they were headed, where they had come from. Joan was startled by the strength of some of these women. One after another, they stood up to reveal shattered lives or families, lost opportunities and hopes. Yet they walked on through life buoyed by an inner sense of optimism and their belief in Christ. These women whose defeats had been devastating, who had no reason to believe in a loving God and understanding Christ, strongly influenced Joan. They fortified her faith in the church and in herself and gave her new tools with which to cope.

When Joan returned home she was still faced with the task of teaching Mary Ellen, whose speech and hearing were excellent, but who was becoming so strong willed that her rebellion went beyond childish tantrums. It took every bit of Joan's energy to maintain control. The daily fights to get Mary Ellen to do her homework continued as usual. So did the hectic rides to the clinic, where Joan was increasingly troubled by Mary Ellen's behavior. Mary Ellen spoke her mind to whomever she pleased, Beebe included. But Beebe would have none of it, and Mary Ellen spent long hours alone in the therapy rooms cooling her fiery temper. Beebe reminded Joan of a Dickens character, a kindly but stern aunt who took no nonsense from her recalcitrant nieces and nephews. The training also got tougher. Beebe would place an object such as a comb among several items on the table in front of Mary Ellen.

"Listen, Mary Ellen. Comb your hair," Beebe instructed from behind Mary Ellen. Beebe expected her to respond to a command, then Beebe moved back several feet and repeated the instructions. She then moved across the room still speaking, expecting Mary Ellen to respond by combing her hair.

The exercise was not over. Beebe's instructions were recorded and played back on tape, requiring even greater concentration. The semi-garbled voice commanded Mary Ellen to comb her hair and repeat various phrases from the tape.

Mary Ellen was developing a fluency in language not usually associated with the deaf, who frequently spoke as though they were reading monotonously from a dictionary.

217

Mary Ellen was speaking in fluid sentences, occasionally missing a word or two but, for the most part, without the former nasal and tongue-tied quality and with close to normal melody. Joan would have a good laugh several years later when a young, impressionable date asked Mary Ellen to identify her accent. Thinking that nearby Philadelphia was the center of the universe, Mary Ellen replied that she hailed from Philly.

Joan had some idea of Mary Ellen's hearing capabilities. She had heard tape recordings at the clinic documenting what it is like to be deaf. The tapes had been electronically doctored to filter out the high frequency sounds, and when they were played the speech was a string of incomprehensible, mumbled words. Beebe's training made this understandable for Mary Ellen. She often followed conversation by listening for certain sounds, usually vowels, and filled in the gaps by deducing what was said. But this is true also of hearing persons. Joan knew of studies that showed hearing people frequently miss as much as 50 percent of what is said to them. They supply the rest by following the context of the conversation.

Even without her aids, there was no such thing as complete silence for Mary Ellen. For one, the training developed her hearing to the point where she was able to discern some sound. And she could "feel" the piano when Joan played in the living room. Without aids, though, her imagination often supplied all kinds of noises she couldn't hear. She "heard" the swoosh of a passing car or the slam of a closing door.

While Mary Ellen's language and hearing were improving, Joan was noticing a slow decline in her schoolwork. Mary Ellen had done well in the first three grades, in part because of the pressure Joan applied on homework. In fourth grade Mary Ellen refused to cooperate. If Joan pushed too hard to get her to study, there was a confrontation. Mary Ellen knew how to thwart her mother.

"You are always asking me to do my homework. Let me do it myself," Mary Ellen frequently argued with Joan.

Joan had no recourse but to back off. But she had enough contact with Mary Ellen's teacher to know that Mary Ellen was not doing her work. When Mary Ellen was caught unprepared in school, she had a stock reply for the teacher: "My mom didn't tell me how to do it."

The teacher was increasingly aware of Joan's frustration and guilt, and though Joan tried to avoid troubling the staff, she was forced to seek out the teacher to discuss Mary Ellen's situation.

"I can't seem to tap her potential," Joan said at one meeting. "Mary Ellen is determined not to do well."

Night and day Joan struggled. She accused herself of laziness, berating herself for not demanding more and expecting better from Mary Ellen. Yet she knew instinctively, as she had all along, the source of the problem. Even the teacher agreed. Mary Ellen was experiencing burn-out. She'd had enough. While her classmates had been in schooling for four years, Mary Ellen was in her eighth year of intensive instruction. She was worn out, as was Joan, and Joan could see it when she tried to get Mary Ellen's attention. Joan's usual procedure was to tap Mary Ellen on the shoulder. Before, Mary Ellen would have turned toward her mother. Now she recoiled.

"Don't touch me. Don't touch me."

Yet each knew she could not give up. Joan was aware that Mary Ellen's future depended on her constant pushing. Joan also knew that Mary Ellen well understood that if she carried her rebellion too far she, not her mother, would be the one to suffer. Joan might push, yank, and pull, but essentially it was Mary Ellen who had to do it, not Joan.

Joan wished Mary Ellen could be like David. He was thriving in school, getting top grades. He was Beebe's model student. The only consolation Joan had was that Claire often found David as difficult as Joan found Mary Ellen. The difference seemed to be that David was a gentleman around Beebe, possibly because he was more intimidated by her than Mary Ellen was. But in his early years David suffered during therapy just as much as Mary Ellen. He would complain of headaches before and after the sessions with Beebe. His sister, Lisa, who thought it too demanding, once pleaded with Claire not to allow David to be treated by the therapists at the clinic. But Claire knew, as Joan knew, that David's salvation depended on the twice-weekly sessions. They had come this far and their children spoke almost perfectly. To stop now would be like dropping out just before the finish line.

If Mary Ellen could not compare to David as a student, she was more at ease among people. She flitted madly about with friends. The summer between fourth and fifth grades, Mary Ellen couldn't wait each day to get down to the pool. She would tear off without companions and take up with any of the children who were having a boisterous time in the water. Joan was pleased by Mary Ellen's outgoing personality. While Mary Ellen was so uninhibited around children her own age, Kathy shied away from new groups and wouldn't go to the pool without a friend or family member.

In fifth grade Mary Ellen firmly established herself as a clown, ready to perform at a moment's notice. If she wasn't cutting up, she was gyrating, bopping and bouncing as a would-be cheerleader. Joan understood the clown personality. She had been and still considered herself one. The

Kennedys never got too serious in life, and Joan carried that tradition into the Huber family. If life became too depressing, they turned to something else. Mary Ellen's cheerleader phase drove Joan mad. If they were in the supermarket, on the street, Mary Ellen and Kathy were clapping and cartwheeling down the aisles and on the sidewalks. And Mary Ellen's deafness had no effect on her ability to scream out the right chants. Little did Joan realize she would have to put up with the cheerleader for several more years.

As Mary Ellen's interest in schoolwork declined further, Joan pondered a solution.

"I think it's time for you to step back a bit," Beebe counseled. She warned that Joan and Mary Ellen were too involved with each other's lives and suggested a tutor who would become the taskmaster, demanding that Mary Ellen take her studies seriously. Twice a week Mary Ellen stayed late at Notre Dame to work on her reading and other studies while Joan prayed somehow she would change her attitude. It wasn't to be. Mary Ellen soon fought the tutor as violently as she fought Joan. At home she steadfastly refused to cooperate, turning away from Joan and even Dick, who was unable to intercede. Joan tried not to trouble Dick with the problems of Mary Ellen. But there were times when it was impossible.

The tutoring continued and in the sixth grade Mary Ellen's performance declined to the point where Joan sought to hire someone to drill Mary Ellen in study skills. But none of the tutors Joan approached had ever instructed a deaf child before. Joan found one woman who reluctantly agreed to take on the task, and Mary Ellen warmed to her immediately.

The woman had a small dog that Mary Ellen adored, and she even looked forward to the lessons twice a week. Joan was almost persuaded that Mary Ellen had reached a turning point.

"Mary Ellen studies beautifully," the tutor told Joan after the first week. "I don't see that she has a problem."

"I only hope it continues," Joan said. "Her track record in new situations like this is two weeks. After that she steadfastly refuses to apply herself." Joan knew that Mary Ellen could be on her best behavior when it suited her, and it was suiting her now.

Within two weeks, however, Mary Ellen was reverting to her old rebellious self. She refused to study, to do the work the tutor expected. At school her performance continued to decline and Joan knew that Mary Ellen was out of her control. Joan spent so much time at Notre Dame talking to teachers, she occasionally was mistaken for a staff member. The sixth grade teacher could do nothing more than Joan.

By the end of the school year, even Beebe was willing to try a new course. Joan and Beebe agreed that Mary Ellen should take the summer off and be free from the constant therapy sessions and the discipline. The change might give her an opportunity to recharge her batteries and go into seventh grade with renewed vigor. But her performance the following year deteriorated and Joan faced the problem of a daughter in adolescence. Mary Ellen had always worn her hearing aids in chest pockets on a vest. But as she developed she tried to hide them. She also grew her hair long to cover up the cords that led to her ears. Joan devised a method of strapping the aids on Mary Ellen's vest just under her arms. Beebe opposed the shift, claiming it would make it difficult for Mary Ellen to hear. But Joan won that round. She knew how important it was for Mary Ellen to feel comfortable around her friends, and she wasn't about to deprive Mary Ellen of the active social life she had developed. If Joan had proved one thing, it was that a profoundly deaf child could grow up to be a normal adult participating in most activities—dating, watching television, going to the movies, and talking on the phone.

There was some consolation that Mary Ellen wasn't the only one of Beebe's students having difficulty about where to locate the hearing aids. David entered seventh grade with trepidation. He, too, wore his aids on his chest and kept his hair long to hide the cords to his ear molds. But David had not yet reached puberty and his voice was still high. He complained to Claire that he wanted the ear-level aids. Beebe was opposed. The ear-level variety were not yet powerful enough, Beebe contended. Pride won out and David began wearing them. Without the new aids he would have been the butt of every junior high joke. David reminded Claire and Beebe that with the chest-level aids looking like developing breasts, his long hair and high voice, he was taken for a girl. Because of his deafness, he still had a slight lisp. And if students knew he was a boy they kidded him about being a homosexual.

For Mary Ellen her studies continued to be her biggest problem. In eighth grade her grades plummeted. Now she was a typical twelve-year-old with a gang of friends, interested in lipstick, mascara, and boys. Her speech was so good that few would have guessed she was deaf. She was able to operate in most situations and was even trying out to be a cheerleader.

Joan was at Notre Dame one day as a volunteer mother when the cheerleader coach, a volunteer like herself, approached.

"I don't know whether Mary Ellen has mentioned this to you, but she has asked to try out to be a cheerleader."

Joan laughed. "She's been dreaming of being a cheerleader for years. Maybe this will get it out of her blood."

"I can't help her," the coach said. "She'll have to make it on her talents and abilities. If she can't, she won't make the group. I'd hate to see her hurt."

"I wouldn't want you to do anything," Joan replied. "She's got to make it on her own. She has to understand her own limits."

Joan worried about Mary Ellen being rejected. As a volunteer mother she had seen her left out or ridiculed by her classmates. Joan knew that some still made fun of her behind her back. She had heard comments some of the children made about Mary Ellen's speech or hearing aids. Joan's instinct was to intercede, but she always fought off the urge. "It's an unforgiving world," she told Dick. "She's got to learn what it's all about. I can't always be there when she needs help."

Joan had seen both Mike and Kathy hurt. It was part of the growing up process and Mary Ellen needed to experience it, too. Still it was difficult for Joan to understand the meaning of deafness. Occasionally Mary Ellen came to her mother, overwhelmed by the struggle to hear and be accepted. Frequently Mary Ellen bore the pain by herself, and Joan had to live silently with her own anguish. She knew she could never fathom the full dimension of being profoundly deaf, even for someone who had overcome the handicap as much as had Mary Ellen. Joan recalled a conversation with Dick.

"I'm always saddened by her deafness," he said. "I think about her when she'll be on her own. How will she hear to get up in the morning? How will she hear when her own children are crying? How much more difficult will her life be because of her deafness? I don't know. She camouflages it well now, but I know it hurts so much. I hope someday she and I can talk about it a little better than we can now."

"You've made it possible for her to be where she is," Joan said.

"Sometimes I stop and daydream about how I would like the world to be," Dick said. "I ask what it would be like if I were wealthy or always blessed with good health. Things like that. If I had just one wish in the world, what would it be? Would I be rich or famous? No. If I had just that one wish, it would be that Mary Ellen would never have been deaf."

There were times when Mary Ellen seemed to need comfort and Joan tried to understand.

"But you don't know what it's like to be deaf," Mary Ellen cried out. "You just don't know what it's like."

The cheerleader tryouts were coming, and Mary Ellen practiced religiously for a place in the lineup. Cheerleaders at Notre Dame held status. If she made the group, she would be envied by the girls and noticed by the boys.

The day for the tryouts arrived, and Joan tried not to think about Mary Ellen's performance. She expected Mary Ellen to do well, as she always did when she was determined. But Joan wondered if Mary Ellen would be able to maintain the cadence, if her voice would be strong enough, or if she could pronounce the words properly. Each girl selected two cheers to be performed before a panel of judges made up of cheerleaders from some of the junior and senior high schools around Allentown.

Mary Ellen came home beaming that afternoon. She had been selected easily while some of the other girls had faltered. Late in the day the telephone rang. It was the coach.

"Mrs. Huber, I just wanted to say that Mary Ellen did superbly today in the cheerleading competition. She was so poised."

"She gets that because she's used to being on the hot seat, expected to perform in her therapy," Joan replied.

"She did marvelously," the coach said. "She got up there in front of all those judges and gave her two cheers." The coach laughed. "She got hung up once or twice and just stopped and asked everyone to wait and then started over again. The judges weren't as interested in how well the cheers came out as they were with the way the girls performed. Some of the girls were so upset they forgot their lines and fled in tears."

Mary Ellen was beyond Joan now. She no longer needed Joan for help and direction as she did when she was a child. Mary Ellen refused to listen, and Joan's prodding only meant more confrontations.

Joan turned to Beebe.

"I don't know what to do with her. She won't study, and if I don't push her she'll fail." Her voice was heavy with fatigue and frustration.

"Let her fail," Beebe shot back.

Joan looked up in surprise.

"Let her fail?"

"Yes," Beebe said. "You've done all you could. Mary Ellen must learn that if she won't apply herself, she'll fail at whatever she is doing. It's time, Joan, for you to step out of her life and for Mary Ellen to mature. She won't like it, but she'll learn."

28

It was a hot day in early June. Joan and Dick, Grandfather, Kathy and Mike sat in the high school auditorium with hundreds of other families. For Mike and Kathy the experience was familiar. They had graduated a few years before from Dieruff, the newer of Allentown's two high schools. The mood was expectant. Mothers and fathers twisted in their seats to catch sight of their sons or daughters. Joan traveled through time as she thought of her own graduation from high school nearly thirty years before. She had seen Mike and Kathy through school, and now it was Mary Ellen's turn. She could remember so many events, so many scenes with Mary Ellen as though they had happened yesterday. She still looked in amazement at her children. They had been infants, then children. Suddenly they were adults with minds and tastes of their own.

Joan smiled. She thought of all the years with Mary Ellen, those days when she was young and helpless, when there was so little hope. Joan plucked random scenes from her memory; when Mary Ellen allowed Kathy to paint her face completely blue. They were no more than three and four. Then there was the time when Joan assumed they were responsible enough to leave alone in the kitchen while she did the wash in the basement. She came upstairs to find Mary Ellen and Kathy squashing pop tarts under the rockers of a rocking chair in the living room. Joan remembered Mary Ellen filling all the kitchen outlets with play dough and the day Dick repaired the roof and Kathy prodded Mary Ellen, hardly more than three, to climb the ladder. Mary Ellen was on her way up when Joan flew out of the house. Later Kathy showed Mary Ellen the secret of getting out of the backyard, to Joan's dismay. She was such a nut, jabbering, always asking questions, stubborn, oh so stubborn. Joan had to laugh at all the nuns Mary Ellen must have driven from the habit during her years in school. They had a separate litany when they dealt with Mary Ellen.

"Mary Ellen, what are you doing now? What are you doing? Mary Ellen, STOP IT!"

If Mary Ellen didn't like someone, including teachers, she told them so. If she didn't feel like reading, she didn't. She was cut from a different cloth, Joan was sure of that.

The graduation ceremonies were about to begin, and Joan was back in the present. Mary Ellen was graduating from high school—proof that Joan's worst fears would not come true. In fact, Mary Ellen had managed respectable C's in high school and remained the same outgoing personality, with many friends, both boys and girls.

The music began, and the 1983 graduates of Dieruff High School began the slow march down the aisles, the boys outfitted in navy blue robes, the girls in gray, the school colors. All the parents were straining to see their own. Joan caught a glimpse of Mary Ellen and fought back her tears. Despite the years of struggle, Joan was overwhelmed with pride.

Mary Ellen had done it. That bull-headed, stubborn little girl always knew she would speak and hear. She just didn't want to make it look too easy. It was Mary Ellen's will that had brought her through just as much as Joan's. Mary Ellen was stunning now, a face upon which eyes would linger.

The graduating seniors took their seats, and the ceremonies began. There were the usual speakers and accolades. The audience waited patiently as selected students rose and walked to the podium for their awards. There would be none for Mary Ellen. Joan felt the irony. If ever someone deserved an honor it was Mary Ellen. The achievements of these top students seemed insignificant compared to what Mary Ellen had accomplished. Joan scanned the seniors and saw Mary Ellen. She turned to Dick:

"Nobody will ever know know the achievement that belongs to that little girl sitting down there. I just wish mom were here to share it."

Postscript

AT TWENTY-ONE MARY ELLEN HUBER is as normal as her many hearing friends. Unconfined by her handicap and feisty as ever, she works at AT&T Technologies in Allentown. Her speech is nearly normal, with some impediments, and her hearing is remarkable. During one-on-one conversations she seldom asks for a statement or question to be rephrased.

The clarity of her speech varies, depending on how much effort she is willing to expend. At times it is difficult to detect any impediment, and she sounds normal. When she is sloppy, Mary Ellen is slightly breathy, as though she had had a cleft palate. Those unused to her speech might assume she was a foreigner and pay closer attention to the conversation. As with all people wearing powerful hearing aids, there is occasional acoustic feedback, a whistling sound from the aid, that can be distracting.

But speech is not the only measure of Mary Ellen's success. Of all Beebe's students she has the most remarkable hearing. Most deaf people are adept at filling in conversational gaps by reading lips, expressions, and body language.

Mary Ellen can carry on a conversation across the room or while not looking directly at her interlocutor.

For Joan, the struggle to bring Mary Ellen into the hearing world ended long ago. All the caveats and dire predictions of doctors, therapists, and educators of the deaf that Mary Ellen would be left without adequate communication skills if she stayed at the Beebe clinic proved unfounded. The warnings that the unisensory method would leave her psychologically scarred and damage family relationships also never came to pass. Kathy works at AT&T. Mike is finishing at the Tyler School of Art in Philadelphia. Dick remains benefits supervisor at AT&T in Allentown, and Joan works as a receptionist in a blood bank in Bethlehem. Grandfather Kennedy, in his late seventies, remains in good health and stops over every day. The Huber family still lives on Troxell Street.

David Davis also has defied the predictions. "I've overcome this handicap of deafness," he says with precise, normal speech. "My therapy was a success and I really don't think about my hearing problem in the course of a day."

Always Beebe's star pupil, David was a top honors student at Easton Area High School and is now a junior at Harvard. David must pay greater attention to the lecture than his fellow students, and frequently approaches the teacher after class for clarification.

When David was discharged from regular therapy sessions at age fifteen, Claire sought new challenges. Today she is a teacher's aide in the Easton Area School District. Jim Davis is senior vice-president and chief financial officer of Easton National Bank and Trust.

Despite Beebe's successes, and Mary Ellen and David are but two, the controversy over the proper method of educating the deaf still rages as violently as before. Witness this recent statement in *The New York Times Book Review*:

"Today a number of previously oral schools for the deaf have changed to "total communication"—signing, oral training, reading, writing, all modes of communication used together to achieve the maximum effect for each pupil. This may be just another swing of the pendulum, but it may also represent the beginning of a truly rational approach to the education of the deaf . . ."

Most educators committed to total communication, with its emphasis on a variety of communications skills, still do not recognize that deaf children can be taught to speak normally. The root of the quarrel between advocates of the unisensory method and total communication is whether deaf children can, in fact, be taught to hear. TC supporters claim that only a few gifted students can achieve this goal.

Bolstered by a growing acceptance of sign language, the influence of TC advocates is increasing. The public's perception is that the deaf are different, unable to enter the hearing world. And this point of view is more firmly embedded every day. Children are exposed to signing on "Sesame Street," interpreters are visible on many television programs, and millions have watched while celebrities like Louise Fletcher and Jane Fonda signed during Academy Awards ceremonies. Beebe fears that reversing the public's acceptance of manual methods of communication may be more difficult in the years ahead than teaching a new generation of deaf children to hear and speak.

To strict oralists like Beebe, total communication denies the deaf child an opportunity to learn to hear and develop normal speech.

"The Total Communication people say they teach children to speak if the child is so inclined, but they put hearing

232

aids on them and then make no effort to develop hearing
and speech," Beebe says. "These kids give in to the line of
least resistance and learn sign language. The average graduate of this system really doesn't have good speech or doesn't
talk at all."

Beebe also believes that TC forces the deaf to mingle almost exclusively with their own kind, and creates a sub-
culture isolated from the mainstream of American society.
She asserts that, all too often, the deaf are relegated to their
own separate world.

Advocates of the unisensory method argue that its very
success accounts for a lack of recognition. Only in recent
years has a clinic like Beebe's been able to introduce graduates who have excellent hearing and speech. But they will
go on to lead normal lives and be assimilated by society.
They are unlikely to join groups lobbying for deaf rights.
The unisensory students have little interest in drawing attention to themselves.

At seventy-six, Helen Beebe remains committed to her
method and the new generations of deaf children who are in
therapy. The enrollment today stands at thirty-four. The
clinic has expanded in recent years and moved around the
corner to more spacious quarters, an old Victorian building
that was converted to combine the clinic, the administrative
offices, and the Larry Jarret House, previously in separate
buildings. Instead of two therapists, the clinic now has five,
including Beebe. In 1981 the clinic hired an executive director and generally there is at least one therapist intern on
the staff.

A critical feature of the clinic today is the Larry Jarret
House, established in 1975 in memory of Larry Jarret, a con-
temporary of Mary Ellen and David, who was killed at age
six in a sledding accident. Many of the families with children

233

enrolled at the clinic do not live in the Easton area and don't have the constant support that was so critical for Joan and Claire. Out-of-town families spend a week there for training and evaluation.

The purpose of Jarret House is to raise parents' expectations and to demonstrate techniques and opportunties to teach their children in a normal home environment. Here therapists observe how a family interacts and become alerted to difficulties that may seem isolated during therapy sessions. For example, one therapist noticed how a mother's unintentional use of eye movement and body language sent such a clear message to her son he did not have to use his hearing.

The clinic also has introduced the senior seminar, a discussion group for older students no longer in need of weekly therapy. Mary Ellen and David both were members. One important objective of the seminar is to train students to address an audience of more than one person and to acquire skills in listening to group conversation.

The clinic also has added the services of a staff psychologist to provide assistance to parents in dealing with the problems of deaf children and to lead an ongoing mothers' support group.

In 1982 the clinic opened a satellite facility in Philadelphia and may open satellites in various other regions in the Northeast to take the unisensory method further afield than Easton. There is even discussion that the Easton center eventually will become strictly an evaluation center while the therapy is conducted at the satellites.

In the years since Mary Ellen Huber was born, technology has transformed the world. In the realm of treating the deaf, however, little has been accomplished. Some small advances have been made in surgical procedures to bring relief to the deaf. Surgeons today are sometimes able to replace or restore the small bones in the middle ear that transmit sound to the cochlea and auditory nerve. They are capable of repairing, even replacing, the eardrum through transplants. Another surgical innovation is a cochlear implant, a device in which a tiny wire is inserted into the cochlea to transmit sounds to the auditory nerve, where they are converted to electrical impulses to be sent to the hearing center in the brain. Several cochlear implant patients have been able to recognize sound, but their ability to distinguish what those sounds are is limited without training. Unisensory advocates argue that no child with residual hearing should be considered for the implant and the implant is of little use to the child who has not acquired at least a minimum of spoken language. Much experience will be required before the full impact of the implants is known.

It is conceivable that the great burden of deafness will have been eradicated a generation or two from now, in the same way that childhood diseases have been wiped out by modern medicine. Until such time, the unisensory method should be seriously considered by any parents who learn they have a deaf child. About 80 percent of unisensory students are mainstreamed, hearing and speaking adults. If there is a drawback, it is in the commitment that is required of the parents. If the mother and father do not have such dedication, the child cannot and will not succeed. But for all the labors, the anguish and frustration, the end result is supremely satisfying. Claire Davis's David attends one of the finest universities in the world. Joan Huber's Mary Ellen is a "normal" young woman who can get on with her life.

Joan's struggle is certainly a triumph of faith, the faith of one woman that her infant daughter someday would lead a normal life, despite the many odds. The story has its parallels. Nearly a hundred years before, another young woman arrived to teach a deaf-mute girl for whom the prognosis seemed hopeless. Decades later, Helen Keller recalled the day Annie Sullivan arrived, to become her teacher and life-long friend.

"Then I came up out of Egypt and stood before Sinai and a power divine touched my spirit and gave it sight so that I beheld many wonders."

So it was for Mary Ellen.

Appendix

Parents who believe their child is deaf and wish to obtain information about the unisensory method may call the Helen Beebe Speech and Hearing Center, Easton, PA., (215) 252–3461. Calls should be directed to Mrs. Beebe or Mrs. Helen Pearson, clinical director. According to Mrs. Pearson, the staff will send appropriate information explaining the unisensory method and the clinic's approach. The information also details steps the family should take to learn the extent of the child's deafness. Mrs. Pearson or Mrs. Beebe will also schedule a clinic visit if the family desires.

Mrs. Pearson stresses that no parent should hesitate to call because of a lack of financial resources. In most cases financial arrangements can be worked out either through a limited number of scholarships or through donations from the family's own community.

Children living close by are placed in therapy twice a week. However, they also can spend several days once or twice a year with their parents at the clinic's Larry Jarret House for intensive therapy.

Families who live too far away for regular therapy sessions are encouraged to visit the Jarret House at least once a year for evaluation. When the therapy is being conducted in their hometown, the therapist is asked to accompany the family on visits to Jarret House to become familiar with the Beebe method.

The Beebe clinic also is headquarters for the Auditory Verbal International Committee (AVI), a group of professional therapists and parents who espouse teaching methods similar to Beebe's. "Auditory Verbal" is the term the committee has selected to cover the various methods similar to unisensory.

To join AVI parents must become members of the Alexander Graham Bell Association for the Deaf in Washington, D.C., the parent body for AVI. A.G. Bell supports the oral method of deaf education and many of its members allow deaf children to learn lip reading while developing their hearing and speech. AVI believes the use of lip reading in the early stages detracts from a child's ability to develop good hearing and speech.

AVI maintains a current list of some thirty professional therapists nationwide who teach the auditory verbal method. In addition, AVI has 400 associate and supporting members, including parents and therapists, who have an understanding or sympathy for the approach even though they may teach other methods besides unisensory or be associated with insitutions that are not strictly auditory verbal.

For additional information about AVI, those interested may call the Beebe clinic or write Mrs. Beebe, 505 Cattell St., Easton, PA 18042, or contact one of the AVI board members listed here.

Helen H. Beebe
505 Cattell Street
Easton, PA 18042
(215) 252–3461 (Work)

608 Porter Street
Easton, PA 18042
(215) 252–6254 (Home)

Nancy Caleffe-Schenck
1544 Lafayette Street
Denver, CO 80218
(303) 871–3658 (Work)

32458 Little Cub Road
Evergreen, CO 80439
(303) 670–0029 (Home)

Warren Estabrooks
Clinical Coordinator
VOICE Auditory Training
  Programme
North York General Hospital
40001 Leslie Street, Three
  South
Willowdale, Ontario
CANADA
(416) 492–3971 (Work)

44 Jackes Avenue, Apt.
  2007
Toronto, Ontario M4T 1E5
CANADA
(416) 961–6883 (Home)

Enelda Luttmann
Sierra Tarahumara 860 Pte.
Lomas Bairilaco
Miguel Hidalgo
Mexico 1000, D. F.
MEXICO
(905) 596–0724 or
  (905) 596–0542

Judy Marlowe
Winter Park Memorial Hospital
200 North Lakemont
  Avenue
Winter Park, FL 32792
(305) 646–7443 (Work)

318 Briarwood Drive
Winter Park, FL 32789
(305) 647–7270 (Home)

Dennis G. Pappas, M.D.
2937 Seventh Avenue
  South
Birmingham, AL
  35233–2991
(205) 251–7169

Helen R. Pearson
505 Cattell Street
Easton, PA 18042
(215) 252–3461

105 Brywood Drive
Easton, PA 18042
(215) 252–2739

239

Doreen Pollack
14285 East Marina Drive
Aurora, CO 80014
(303) 755–3694

Ellen Rhoades
AEC, Incorporated
3016 Lanier Drive
Atlanta, GA 30319
(404) 237–6141 (Work)

856–5 St. Charles Avenue
Atlanta, GA 30306
(404) 876–4063 (Home)

Judy Simser
Aural Habilitation Supervisor
Audiology Department
Children's Hospital of
 Eastern Ontario
401 Smyth Road
Ottawa, Ontario
(613) 737–2378 (Work)

24 Pentland Crescent
Kanata, Ontario K2K 1V5
CANADA
(613) 592–1373 (Home)

Dr. Gordon Stanfield
121 Linda Drive
Biloxi, MS 39531
(601) 388–3343

Box 4673
Biloxi, MS 39531
(601) 388–1376 (24-hour
 answering)

Keesler Medical Center
ENT
(601) 377–6911 (let ring)
8:00 A.M.–11:00 A.M., 1:30
P.M.–4:00 P.M.

Dr. Joseph Stewart
Department of Health and
 Human Services
Indian Health Services
Sensory Disabilities
 Program
2401 12th Street, N.W.
Albuquerque, NM 87102

Sally Tannenbaum
3336 Wade Street
Los Angeles, CA 90066
(213) 398–4744

Maxine Turnbull
2453 La Jolla Drive
Tempe, AZ 85282
(602) 839–6657 (Home)
(602) 820–8817 (Work)